Major General sir Henry worsley, 1768 - 1841
Benefactor to Chale School
Inscription Reads:
"Major General Sir Henry Worsley, GCB, who presented Eleven hundred Pounds for the Promotion of
the objects of the Royal Asiatic Society." (Bust stands in entrance hall R.A.S., London.)

A Particularly Happy Little School

Local historians are renowned for researching a subject for years, possibly a lifetime, and never writing it up. The excuse usually is that there is just this one more vital piece of information needed before the book can be written, one can happily research for ever. However, the definition of an essay I have been told is "a report of work in progress". The work presented here is just that. The more I have delved into Chale school's history the more there is to find out.

I have to thank the many people who have helped me in this project. The Headteacher and governors at the school have given me a free run of all the records available there. Local residents (too many to name individually) and former pupils and staff further afield have most willingly shared their memories, their photographs and other memorabilia. The Isle of Wight Record Office, the Church of England Record Office and the Diocesan Education Office have all been very helpful, as also have various Departments at I.W. County Hall. The Isle of Wight Teachers' Centre allowed me to use their library. Without the co-operation of all these people the task would have been impossible. My thanks also to Mari Nicholson and Joan Waddleton who have read the manuscript and made many helpful suggestions. Lastly I thank my friends and relatives who have put up with my obsession over nearly a decade.

Whether village schools such as this one survive through the 21st century is always in doubt. Should Chale school fall victim to reorganisation and cut-backs I hope this book will keep alive memories of "A Particularly Happy Little School".

Dorothy Wright   2002

A PARTICULARLY HAPPY LITTLE SCHOOL

ϙ

A History of the village school at Chale, Isle of Wight

By
Dorothy Wright

(Ref: School Log Book, 2 May 1947; "This is a particularly happy little school....It is a great pleasure to visit the school and to converse with such responsive and well-informed pupils." Canon T. Grigg-Smith, Director of Religious Education.)

Published by Fernlea Publications 2002

ISBN
0-95-19122-6-7

iii

A Particularly Happy Little School

List of Illustrations

CONTENTS

A Particularly Happy Little School

CHAPTER 1

Before and soon after the Beginning

The small community of Chale existed for hundreds of years with no thought of universal education. Then the stirrings of change, and the growth of the Industrial Revolution brought the idea of teaching everyone. It reached even this remote hamlet on the Isle of Wight, and though no school existed in 1790, the very first suggestion of one had been hinted at 200 years before. In 1608[1] a fragment of information, only a line in a list of Laymen's Licences of the Diocese of Winchester, revealed that this small settlement had an unlicensed schoolmaster, named English in that year. Education for the poor of Chale does, however, date from the end of the eighteenth century, some 50 years before the building of today's school.

In 1788 it is recorded that 353 people lived in the village[2] and no doubt they endured real hardship in the winter from cold and hunger. Many were farm labourers, others provided the necessary services of baking, brewing, shoe mending, undertaking and so on. Yet others earned their keep from the sea, by fishing, smuggling, wrecking and gathering flotsam. Wages, if any, amounted to shillings rather than pounds.

As a bedtime prayer at Chale children were taught:

"God bless Daddy, God bless Mammy!
Come wind, come storm,
Wreck ashore before morn!"[3]

Wreckage from sea disasters could then have meant survival for poor folk and the prayer was not as heartless as it may appear. Collecting spoil from wrecks supplemented income.

Life was not easy, unstable cliffs collapsed, and the coast eroded. Sometimes excessive rain brought floods from the Downs, while fierce gales caused havoc among the crops and spelt disaster. Shipwreck and drowning were daily hazards. In the good times fertile fields, plentiful Downland grazing and the harvest from the sea made life bearable.

The school's history is paralleled in many rural areas across England, and catalogues not only development and change in education over the years, but also life in the community. Documents from churches, local Diocesan Education Offices, County Archives and the school itself reveal how schooling became available to every child. The route was complex, confused and as full of argument and dissension as it is today. Education had long been available to the few who could pay but for most people was, quite literally, a closed book. The change began in the late eighteenth century, though another hundred years was to pass before school attendance became compulsory.

Growing industrialisation saw an explosion of population, and one of the reasons for the shift in ideas was that Church dignitaries saw a vast number of children growing up quite ignorant of the Apostles' Creed, and the Catechism (both to be found in the Book of Common Prayer) and unable to read Bible stories. Their concern centred around teaching children to read, principally so they could learn more from the Bible and become good members of the established Christian Church (i.e. the Church of England).

Chale's rector in the late 18th century was the Reverend Francis Worsley, a member of the wealthy and influential local family who had promoted free schooling on the Isle of Wight since the sixteenth century. Following in his ancestors' footsteps, he was a great supporter of education for the poor. In his visitation returns for 1788 he reported "No school". Nevertheless people both locally and all over the country were thinking about schooling for all. Many were leaving bequests to their community to found a school, and Chale had three such benefactors.

The first was Robert Weekes, who died in December, 1788. In his will he left the sum of £150[5][i] to Chale with instructions that this be invested in government stock and the yearly interest used to pay a "poor indigent woman" to teach children of the parish to "read the English tongue". Girls were also to be taught knitting and needlework. The money was invested in the Isle of Wight House of Industry (another name for the Workhouse) which was being built at the time. Two bonds, one for £100 and the other for £50, were bought. Interest on these was "to be applied by the minister and churchwardens of Chale in pursuance of the directions of his (Robert Weekes) will".

The second came from John Barber, who died in 1796. He gave the parish £200 with much the same instructions. The minister and churchwardens of Chale were to invest the bequest, but they had to appoint a schoo<u>master</u>, who was to be maintained on the interest. His task was to teach the children to read and<u>write</u>, and instruct them in the church catechism. If at any time no suitable teacher could be found, the trustees were to use the money "in acts of charity amongst such poor persons of the parish of Chale as they should think fit subjects for relief". Investment was made in "three per cent consols"[8] (i.e. Consolidated Annuities) held in the names of the rector, Rev. Francis Worsley, and William Jolliffe, churchwarden of Chale. As other people were appointed to these offices, so the holders of the shares were changed[9]. Dividends were paid into a bank in Newport, 8 miles distant. These two bequests founded what was to become known as Chale Charity School. Whether the very first teacher appointed at Chale was man or woman is not recorded, it is possible a married couple was chosen, the man to teach the boys, his wife to instruct the girls (in order to adhere to the conditions). No qualifications were called for - no recognised elementary teaching qualifications existed. The standard of

[i] He left a similar sum for the same use to the neighbouring parish of Niton.

instruction can, therefore, only be guessed at, and was undoubtedly very low. In some cases the job was given to a poor person who was unable to earn a living any other way, perhaps through disability or age. Sometimes, of course, dedicated teachers emerged and children were inspired to learn, and Chale seems to have been fortunate in attracting its share of these.

The custom was for school teachers of the time to work in their own home, not always at the village centre. Very often this also meant crowded conditions in poorly furnished, dark, damp and cold cottages. Sometimes the children had to stand for lack of benches. Perhaps it was with this in mind that the third person to assist education in Chale was the Rev. Francis Worsley himself.

He and his brother, the Reverend James Worsley of Stenbury, I.o.W., were friends of the Chale benefactor John Barber, and acted as his executors. Worsley, therefore, was already much involved with the idea of teaching poor people to read and write. He served as rector to the parish for 55 years, from 1753 until his death in 1808. In a codicil to his will he left instructions that the schoolmaster was to teach the poor children reading, writing and arithmetic. He also said that a cottage called Goodalls, on the far western edge of the parish (of which he held the lease)[iii] was to be the residence of the schoolmaster free of rent. In addition a detached moveable school-room, erected there, was to be used "for the more convenient instruction of the poor children of the said parish".

Worsley's generosity extended further as he also provided £5.00 annually, part of his income from Rookley Farm (which he owned) to pay for the yearly painting and maintenance of the school-room, and any necessary repairs to the school-house. What surplus remained at the end of the year was to be given to the schoolmaster for "the bettering of his salary". As if all that was not enough, the Rev. Worsley said that when he no longer held the lease of Goodalls, the Minister and Churchwardens were to use the £5 to rent another suitable house and take the school-room to it.[ii]

The house was already in use as the master's residence in 1800[iii]. A receipt dated February 18th of that year states that William Dash, then living at Goodalls, received the sum of eight pounds seven shillings and three pence being half a year's salary as Master of the School[11].

By 1811 the population of Chale has increased to 406, and the school contained "40 to 60 children", which suggests that the schoolroom may have been rather crowded. The Master's annual salary was £16 14s. 6d, dividends from the

---

[ii] No description of the latter remains, apart from the memory of an elderly resident who said that she saw it in 1924, that "it stood on stones", and was about the size of a wooden army hut. It appears to have been located on a small flat area across the lane from Goodalls. Perhaps it could be dismantled for removal, and maybe Chale had the very first mobile classroom. When it was actually demolished has not been discovered.

[iii] The cottage, modernised and enlarged, still stands today.

investments mentioned above (no increase since William Dash signed for his half year's pay). "School pence" were also charged, and this amount, together with the Rector's bounty, would have boosted the Master's wages. A Select Committee report on the Education of the Poor (1818) stated that in Chale "The poor do not possess sufficient means of education, but are very anxious to have them"[2].

By this time education of the poor had become a subject for discussion in Parliament. Hitherto the State took no part in providing this, considering it something religious and other philanthropic organisations gave as a "voluntary" service. Indeed many schools were called voluntary schools, and the title still exists - to-day Chale is a "voluntary controlled Church of England Primary school" (more of the "controlled" part later, see page 73).

Religion was very important at that time and in the early years it did seem that the teaching of poor children was to be entirely the responsibility of the Church. An attempt in 1807 to establish schools by an Act of Parliament, failed because the education to be offered did not have a totally religious basis, and was not securely in the hands of the minister of each parish. In 1820 another attempt was made with a bill that sought to require all teachers to prove they were members of the Church of England. Dissenters raised a storm of protest at this, resulting in another failure. So began a long battle between various Churches over rights to organise education, and over the curriculum offered.[iv]

In the early nineteenth century, more and more children required education as the population continued to expand and the Churches and other voluntary bodies found they just could not cope. There was inadequate space in existing buildings, and it was impossible to raise sufficient money to extend them. Neither could teachers be found for the vast number of pupils. Eventually, in 1832, after much discussion and argument, the Government set aside £20,000 for public education, and thus began state aid to education. The amount became an annual grant and increased rapidly from then on.

At first use of this money was to be confined to erecting new schools, and application for a share had to be made through either the National Society or the British & Foreign Schools Society (see page 5). Other strings were attached, too. Schools so aided had to agree to government inspection, they had to conform to certain standards of construction, and thirdly the building had to be secured by a Deed of Trust (see page 8) dedicating it as a school for the poor forever. Following a national inquiry into the state of education in 1837 a committee of the Privy Council was set up to investigate education of the poor.

[iv]) The problems continue to this day with other religions besides Christianity (e.g. Moslem, Hindus, Jews) involved. In addition the secular position is nowadays put very forcefully.

The population of Chale was increasing as everywhere else, and by then stood at 544[13]. The school at Goodalls had 55 pupils, 35 boys and 20 girls, 38 of these children received free tuition, the others being paid for by their parents at 1d or 2d per week.

Non-conformism must have arrived in Chale in the mid-eighteenth century when the fervour of the Wesley brothers penetrated remote parts of the Island and had strong support. The Rev. Worsley's visitation returns of 1788 again give information definitely stating "No Chapels". Nevertheless the house of James Nobbs at Chale was listed as a licensed Dissenter Meeting House[14], and Wesleyan Methodists started a Sunday School in Chale in the early eighteen hundreds[5]. By 1823, 30 children were receiving free instruction on Sundays in a schoolroom built for the purpose (still standing opposite the Chapel to-day). The local Church of St Andrews, meanwhile, similarly catered for 35 pupils (also gratuitously). The 10 children additional to the day-school pupils probably worked all week on farms, and could only go to school on Sunday. It was usual, too, for the working children to be taught reading and writing that day as well as Bible stories, and in schools under C. of E. influence, the creed, the ten commandments and the catechism (Book of Common Prayer) . Mention is made of a lending library at St Andrews, suggesting that adults, too, were becoming involved in learning to read.

Surprisingly the 1818 Select Committee Report on the Education of the Poor found that most children started school at two years of age, and at one or two places in Hampshire (which then included the Isle of Wight) they were as young as 18 months[16]. The report also said that some leave at 7 years of age (perhaps when they had reached an age to be helpful at home), "while others remain after that - even after 14 years". Maybe parents working long hours themselves looked on school as an early child-minding service, and reasons for staying on could have been many. Possibly these children were unable to be employed in the usual way owing to mental or physical handicap. Or they were the bright ones taken on at a small wage to assist the teacher.

All schools in the County of Southampton were open to all children regardless of their parents' religious denomination[17]. Roman Catholics had long suffered exclusion from Universities, and from holding public office, and none had the right to vote, their rights being also the subject of intense discussion at this time. Neither did the Establishment readily accept Free Church supporters. Allowing all denominations into Church Schools represented, therefore, a considerable advance, and points to concern for all children's needs, though it must be said C. of E. doctrine was emphasised, much to the displeasure of other denominations. Nevertheless parents of such children had to wait until the important Education Act of 1870 (see page 20) to gain the right to withdraw their children from religious instruction classes.

Chale eventually followed events of the time by becoming a National School, or (to give it its full name) a member of the National Society for Promoting the Education of the Poor in the Principles of the Established Church throughout

England and Wales[18]. This Society had been founded in London in 1811, and used the teaching methods of an early educationalist, the Rev. Andrew Bell. The system was soon taken up on the Isle of Wight, a school in the principal town (Newport) joining within twelve months, and others soon following. Chale churchmen must have been familiar with the National Society's system long before their school became a member. By 1831 there were 13,000 National Schools, many of these being both day and Sunday schools and more than 400,000 children attended them[19].

Bell was not the only educator of the poor in that period. Another society came into existence in London as the non-conformists and other denominations were challenging the Church of England. Called the British & Foreign Schools Society (originally the Royal Lancasterian Institution), it was founded by a young Quaker named Joseph Lancaster[20]. He was considered to be the instigator of interdenominational religious schooling, he accepted pupils from all sects and taught only doctrine common to all Christian people. (The "Foreign" part of the title merely records that Lancaster's methods spread beyond the United Kingdom to the Colonies, Europe and the Americas, as indeed did those of the National Society.)

Both societies used the monitorial system, by which a teacher taught the older children, termed "monitors", who then passed on the knowledge to small groups of younger pupils. It was obviously not an ideal method, and much learning was done mechanically and by rote.

In many parts of the country, though, it became evident that charities intended to support schools, or make other provision for the poor, were being misdirected. Chale does not seem to have been so affected, nevertheless the village's charities were included in a general Commission of Enquiry set up in 1816 to document such gifts and make sure they reached those for whom they were intended[21]. The report of this commission was published 20 years later, and led to the founding in 1853 of the present well-known Charities Commission.

Far from the centre of argument Chale children trudged 1, 2 and sometimes 3 miles to the Charity School at Goodalls in all weathers. No further record of these early years has been uncovered until events brought a big change in 1841.

---

[v] A list of Chale's Charities appears on an ancient board hung in the school's entrance hall.

CHAPTER 2

A New School - thanks to Sir Henry

Francis Worsley held Goodalls' lease with two of his sons, James and Henry, who both died in 1841, Sir Henry in January and his brother in March. A lease was often held for a term of 99 years, or "on three lives", i.e. father, son and grandson. With the low life expectancy of the times this was likely to average out to about 33 years apiece. When the last named died the agreement ended, even if less than 99 years had elapsed. So suddenly the master's house and the site of the school room had gone. What was to be done? As Chale school had become a valued part of village life, attention was urgently turned to provision of new premises.

Fortunately Chale had yet another benefactor, Major General Sir Henry Worsley, son of Rev. Francis. A man of some distinction, as his memorial in Chale Church records:-

> "At the early age of thirteen he carried arms in the cadet company at Fort St George, Madras and for many years held the situation of Adjutant General in Bengal with honor (sic), zeal and ability. Distinguished in numerous brilliant engagements; Munificent in donations to public institutions; charitable, generous, unostentatious, he was ever ready to relieve the afflicted, to comfort the orphan and the widow. In him the poor lament the death of a benefactor and the Indian Army mourns the loss of one of its brightest ornaments.

He was certainly generous as he provided handsomely in his will for his 5 illegitimate children[22][vi]. His munificence included in 1828 the donation of £300 "for the aid and support of Chale Charity School", and this eventually paid for the building of to-day's school[23]. Again, 11 years later, on 10 April 1839, Sir Henry provided £166.13s.4d., and the interest from this amount was "to be expended on Books for children and surplus in Bread for the Children or Aged Persons of Chale"[24]. Both amounts were invested in 3% Consols, and for many years thereafter bread was distributed in school just before Christmas.[vii]

[vi] This supposes Sir Henry was a philanderer. However, further information suggests that the mother of all these children was his housekeeper, whom he married just a few years before his death. Possibly she was already married, divorce was not an option, and they had to await her husband's decease before marrying.
[vii] Throughout England at this time wealthy people gave money for schools, sometimes in a lump sum, sometimes by means of a legacy, and often as an annual subscription. Others, not quite so affluent, gave gifts in kind, perhaps vegetables to

Towards the end of his life Sir Henry wrote to a new rector of Chale, the Rev. Andrew Gother, inviting him to become trustee of the school[5]. He said "it would be very gratifying to me at this Eleventh Hour of my Pilgrimage, to know that the Parish School at Chale and the funds for its support were in the best possible train to Insure its Prosperity and Perpetuity". His letter also implies that he expected the £300 he gave in 1828 to grow so that in time it would provide "increased means...to build, purchase or rent a good and suitable House for all the purposes of the School". He realised that very soon the deaths of himself and his brother would mean the expiry of the lease at Goodalls and the school would have to be moved.

In 1843 land was given, a Deed of Trust[viii] was signed and building commenced.

As a trustee the Rev. Gother took his duties seriously, and he must have felt that the children's education was being carried on too far from his jurisdiction. The pupils were being brought up in the traditions of the Church of England, and were expected to attend Church regularly. The rector also saw it as his duty to supervise the teaching of the creed and catechism. When the Charity School was at Goodalls, some 1½ miles from the centre of the parish and with poor road access, this was inconvenient in both respects.

School buildings all over the country were about to take a place at the centre of their communities. Together with the Church and the Inn, the school completed the triangle of public buildings that still identify the typical English village. In Chale, St Andrew's Church and the Wight Mouse Inn had long been neighbours. When the time came to move the school, no doubt in consultation with the churchwardens and other influential residents, the rector looked for a site close to the church (the proximity of the pub perhaps being seen as a regrettable coincidence!).

Many parishes had major landlords, perhaps members of the aristocracy, local squires, or other wealthy residents. These people often gave land for a school. Chale, however, had no such rich patrons. Glebe land (i.e. land included in a clergyman's benefice) existed and the Rev. Gother offered to set aside a portion of this for the purpose. As it was not personally his to give, permission had to be sought from the Bishop of Winchester, in whose diocese the village lay[6].

When this was received a Deed of Trust[7] was prepared which stated (in the usual long-winded legal fashion) that the rector did:

---

supplement the teacher's salary, wood for the school fire, or even stone and work-hours to construct the building.

[viii] A Deed of Trust was a legal document naming three parties: (a) the donor of the gift; (b) the holders (or trustees) of the gift; and (c) the beneficiaries of the gift (in this case the school and its pupils).

"freely and voluntarily and without any valuable consideration grant and convey unto the Minister Churchwardens and Overseers of the poor of the said parish and their successors All that piece or parcel of glebe land or ground situate lying and being in the said parish of Chale containing by admeasurement half an acre."

This, it said was part of a field known as "the Vicar's Butt and garden...". The Deed went on to say that all buildings on it or to be erected on it were to be "for ever hereafter appropriated and used" as a school for the education of poor children, and a residence for the school master or mistress. The teaching was to be according to the principles of the National Society, and a management committee of subscribers (probably the forerunners of the Board of Managers) was to be set up. In addition the school should be open at all times to inspectors "as appointed in conformity with Her Majesty's Order in Council" dated 10 August 1840.

The Deed was signed on 25 September 1843 by the rector, churchwardens (William Hatcher Barton and William Lambert Deacon), and overseers (William Hillier and David Brown), all in the presence of "Abraham Baker, Schoolmaster, Chale, IW". The Rectors of the nearby parishes of Niton and Calbourne, and the Vicar of Shorwell also signed to say that they had inspected the land, agreed the size and ascertained that it was close to the church. Once these formalities were completed the school was then said to be "in Union with the National Society", and prepared to abide by its system and rules.

One of these rules was that all children in the National Society schools "without exception, (be) instructed in this Liturgy and Catechism and... they do constantly attend Divine Service in their Parish Churches and other places of public worship under the Establishment, wherever the same is practicable on the Lord's Day"[28]. This was to cause many problems when children of parents belonging to other denominations attended a voluntary school in the hands of the Church of England.

Construction work was in progress early in the year, the estimate "To Build a School at Chale I of W according to the accompanying Plans and Specifications" being dated 16 March 1843 (Appendix 2). Messrs William Way & Son, of Newport, IW, (possibly related to the Ways who lived in the parish) undertook the building[29]. Their price for excavating foundations, building a "Boy's (sic) School Room", a "Girl's (sic) School Room", the residence and various small outhouses came to £405.6s.5 3/4d. "If Stone quoins[iv], and stones round all windows and Doors in outside excepting the Privies, round Wood house Door, and window over; add Six Pounds to the above amount." In early December of the same year, the Rev. Gother

---

[iv] Quoins - the external corners of walls.

handed over £405.0s.0d.[30], the bulk of which must have come from the 1828 gift of Sir Henry Worsley (see page 7).

In money terms today (1996) this would be the equivalent of about £13,000, and the price sounds reasonable enough considering how small and simple the building was, in no way approaching the standards now required. The specification stated "All stones to be delivered on the ground by the Rev. A W Gother free of any expense to the Builder". Since the price paid is slightly less than that quoted, did the rector and his parishioners provide other materials, too, or earn a discount for prompt payment? The stone quoins are still visible but apparently the extra £6 for them was not paid.

Solicitors' fees for preparing the conveyance, getting the approval of the Education Committee of the Privy Council, expenses in procuring various signatures and other incidentals amounted to £8.11s.6d[31]. The Rev. Gother was presented with this account at the end of the year.

The masons had been instructed to "Run cement Tablet in Front for an inscription". This, also still in place, reads "CHALE PAROCHIAL SCHOOLS 1843". Though the use of the plural may seem strange it was the custom to keep the sexes separate with a schoolroom and entrance for each. In some cases "Mixed Infant" rooms were also provided and had their own door. Chale's boys occupied the room on the south of the master's house, and the girls used the one on the north. So Chale's present school building was established without any contribution from the National Society. At this time, too, it changed its name from Charity School to Voluntary School, while also becoming a National School. Running expenses continued to be met by dividends from the original bequests, school pence, and by subscriptions and donations from the local community.

The school then entered its second phase situated opposite the church and pub, and within a few hundred yards of the rectory. Abraham Baker, moved into the new house with his wife Ann, and his two daughters[32], one of whom (also named Ann) was his assistant. The other, Sarah, still only 12 in 1843, and possibly one of the pupils, was to become a village dressmaker.

Details of the numbers on roll at the time are not available, but the census records for 1841 and 1851 show a large number of children in the area. The occupations of the adults remained centred round farms and fishing with a smattering of associated craft workers (blacksmiths and masons), and domestic providers such as bakers, shoemakers and servants. Coastguards, too, from their cottages at Blackgang and Atherfield, came and went, sending their children during their stay to Chale school.

For some 14 years the school remained unchanged, and then in 1857 an Infant Room was added[33]. Whether this was required due to a further increase in population, or was seen as a necessity to cater for young children who otherwise suffered as their mothers went out to work, or maybe to help keep older sisters at school, is not known.

In whatever circumstances the plans were drawn up showing the new room as an extension to the east through the Girls' School. With thick stone walls, slate roof and board floor, it matched the other classrooms in size. An external door on the East, two windows and a "Gallery" were provided. This latter meant tiered seating (similar to a modern lecture hall) on one side of the room. How the teacher managed to persuade tiny children to remain there is a mystery. Perhaps by squashing them in tightly and brandishing a cane.

The estimated cost was £94.10s (equivalent to £5,500 by 1992 rates), and there a problem arose. Only £87.10s was forthcoming from "Subscriptions and collections raised in the locality", leaving a balance of £7 for "fittings and sundries". There was only one way of finding this - to apply to the National Society for a grant[4]. The Reverend A W Gother sent in an Application (No. 1407) on 25 June 1857 and within a month the money was granted. At the end of July a letter of thanks was sent, together with a statement, signed by Rector and Churchwardens, saying the work was completed "in a satisfactory and workmanlike manner". All subscriptions had been paid, the full debt cleared, and a Balance Sheet was enclosed. A note also said that a further subscription of one guinea (£1.5p.) had been received[5].

With this extra room the school was then said to be able to provide accommodation for all children in the parish. 37 infants (at a fee of 1d each per week) were expected which meant a considerable increase in pupil numbers. Another question on the application form concerned available church accommodation for the proposed numbers in school. The answer was "Sufficient", confirming the intention of taking the children regularly to church. This extension increased the school area by 1/3, which proved adequate for another 30 years.

Though this particular school's records are minimal until 1869, in England as a whole much educational discussion, controversy and eventual progress continued. When the government raised the annual grant to £39,000, it had been intended also to set up a training college for teachers. This would have brought such training under the state, and, therefore, the Established Church of England. Great religious antagonism arose again over this and the idea had to be abandoned, teacher-training remained in private hands, with most children being taught by the inefficient monitorial method.

In the same year that Chale's new school was built the Committee of Council decided to make grants for the building of training colleges (called Normal Schools). These were intended for prospective teachers in both National Schools and those of the British and Foreign Schools Society, so making them interdenominational. From the very early days of the National Society, teacher-training had been offered under the Rev. Dr Andrew Bell, and a "Society of School Masters upon the Madras System under the patronage and protection of the National Society" was in existence. (The Madras System was another name for the monitorial system, perhaps Sir Henry had come across it during his service in that state.)

Improvement in the quality of teaching took another step forward three years later when in 1846 the system of pupil-teachers was introduced[36]. Promising pupils were selected to remain at school for about 5 years beyond the usual age of leaving. They worked under a headteacher, from whom they were supposed to receive individual instruction for 1½ hours daily (depending on how conscientious the teacher was). During the usual school hours they assisted in the schoolroom. Gradually further advances were made, so the pupil-teachers received a small wage, and there was the opportunity to gain a Queen's scholarship to go on to training college in due course.

Finance still remained a worry for many schools. Voluntary donations and regular subscriptions could not meet all necessities. A scheme for capitation grants (of 3s [15p] to 6s [40p]per head) for rural areas was introduced by the Committee of Council in 1853. These were only given provided the school had a certificated teacher, that three quarters of the pupils passed an examination, and that voluntary contributions and school pence still matched the grant. Whether Chale's master, Abraham Baker, was suitably qualified is not known. The 1882 school accounts (the first available) included an entry under "Grant from Committee of Council on Education", amounting to £73.5s.[37], and George Amos (who took over in that year) was very clever and highly likely to be qualified (see page24).

The annual Parliamentary contribution for education continued to rise. In 1851 it reached £150,000 and only 7 years later came to £663,400 (by then including provision for the capitation grant as well as building). There was still argument between those who felt schooling should remain in the private "voluntary" system, and others who wanted the state to have full control. Through the urgings of both factions a Royal Commission of Enquiry was set up under the Duke of Newcastle (the Newcastle Commission). Its 5 volume report was issued in 1861, covering every aspect of education. The section on rural schools is most relevant to the present story.

The situation concerning school endowments reported some misappropriation. Though Chale's charities seem to have been correctly applied, where malpractice occurred some gifts were regarded as "being utterly ineffective for the purposes of education" and "repressing all local liberality and energy, and standing in the way of any improvement".

One of the schools particularly mentioned in this respect was that at Sydling St Nicholas, in Dorset. It is of interest because Chale's benefactor John Barber was born there, and left £500 to provide a local school with the same instructions as for Chale[38]. What could have gone wrong? It is possible that correct application of a charity depended entirely on personalities, and perhaps those involved with Sydling St Nicholas were careless, or not educated enough themselves to be able to cope. Nevertheless investigation in 1993 showed that this charity still thrives, yielding some £200 per year, while Chale's returns dwindled to almost nil.

Across the country problems with charities arose because the money was specifically for the wages of the teacher, which meant it could not be used for books etc. for the pupils' use. The master also lived in a tied schoolhouse and it was no-one's responsibility to dismiss him, neither would he retire if he became old and ill as he had nowhere else to go and no other money. Sometimes the rector himself took on the duties of schoolteacher, and then concentrated his efforts on private paying pupils, leaving the poor children to his curate, while still drawing full wages from the endowment for himself.

Buildings, according to the Report, were often dilapidated, even ruinous, as endowments catered only for the teacher's salary. Chale, of course, had the regular £5 from Francis Worsley to maintain its property. Untrained teachers worked in schools where the number of children was too low for a certificated teacher to be affordable. It was allowed, however, that a fair number of these teachers were intelligent and doing duty with "a creditable amount of skill and success". Apathetic trustees, accounts not made public, and it being no-one's duty to remonstrate with a master for dereliction of duty were other complaints regarding endowed rural schools.

The poor state of education was also connected with the attitudes of parents, pupils and employers. The Commission found that country children were unlikely to remain at school beyond 10 years old for boys and 12 years "at the outside" for girls. As prospective farm workers it was considered that the boys had much to learn (ploughing, thatching, care of animals etc), and needed to start as early as possible. Girls, of course, were required to help at home with younger children, learn domestic arts and possibly free the mother to take paid employment. The parents saw no reason for lengthy schooling for their off-spring when they could earn a few shillings towards their keep. As for employers, when they hired an agricultural labourer this sometimes meant a claim also on the labour of his family. With the farm cottage being tied to the job the man was powerless to refuse.

The need for regularity was not easy to instil either, but non-attendance often meant the loss of capitation grant. The Committee of Council had decided that a child should be at school for a minimum of 176 days per annum to qualify, a fairly low attendance rate considering school was open for 44 weeks, 5 days a week (sometimes 5½). When they did come, children were not always punctual. Few labourers owned watches so how could they be if they were out of earshot of church or stable clock? Parents were not too concerned about this, and the teacher found he had to educate the whole family in the need for regularity and timeliness.

Discipline raised yet another difficulty. Often parents were according to the report "very touchy" regarding punishment. They corrected their children by a blow in the passion of the moment, as they would correct puppies. For a child to be caned for lateness, untidiness, lack of personal cleanliness and a hundred other small social graces now taken for granted, seemed to them deliberate, premeditated and very cruel (which in some cases it may have been).

There is no way of knowing whether any of this happened at Chale. Log books for the period do not survive (if indeed any were kept). Disciplinary problems are likely to have existed, certainly later records confirm this, the cane was in use at the school well into living memory. The first log book available is dated 1869[9], though they were compulsory for grant-aided schools from 1862. Even though instructions for keeping these include "No reflections or opinions of a general character are to be entered...", the feelings, attitudes and abilities of the teachers come through clearly and build up an excellent picture of Victorian rural school life. This regular journal of day to day events reflects changes in education as the state continued to expand its role.

The author of the Report on rural schools (the Rev. James Fraser) clearly felt that education should continue to be based on religious principles. He said "Personal influence - the presence of some one loving heart and fostering hand - is the true lever: that creates and maintains the efficiency of a school. This fact alone appears to me to demonstrate the impossibility of merely secular education as the basis of a national system". In 1861 the Church of England's fight for the schools (and the hearts and minds of the children) was obviously active and on-going. The Commission as a body rejected the idea of free and compulsory schooling, mainly due to what had become known as the "religious difficulty".

As a result of the Newcastle report a grant system known as "Payment by Results", or the Revised Code, was introduced. It was really prompted by the deficiencies found in teaching, and to make sure the teachers were doing good work. Every child in schools receiving a government grant was to be presented for examination, to see if they really were being taught satisfactorily. For every child qualifying for a grant on the old system 4s.(20p) per annum was to be paid, and for those who passed the examination a further amount (up to 8s.[40p]) could be awarded. Though modifications were brought in over the ensuing years, it was not until 1904 that payment by results was finally abolished.

The system must have been very difficult for the teachers who, even if they were trained, were using poor teaching methods (according to today's thinking). The pupils, too, were not able to assimilate the knowledge for many reasons, not least poor home conditions, poor nutrition, and possibly physical disabilities (e.g. hearing and visual defects). Certainly the system was very unpopular with teachers, and can be compared with the modern equivalents of parental choice of school and publication of examination results. The idea was to weed out inefficient schools, but local conditions were not taken into consideration, and much unfairness resulted.

Chale's log book records a "general examination" in December 1870 when the Standards (or classes) were intermixed to prevent copying, but it is not clear whether this was for the award of extra grants under the Code. In 1871 three children moved with their parents to Cowes, their education standard recorded as "fit for Exam". A note of panic in 1872 suggests the importance of the examination. Easter holidays were put off because "the examination being so near (16 April)...the children readily consented to come to school and have their holidays at some future time". The conducting of the event seemed fairly unofficial, however, as on one occasion the teacher added "The arithmetic papers very neatly done and most of the sums right in upper Standards, the Dictation was also an improvement upon their past work in both III, IV and V Standards". Regular school tests were apparently held each week as can be understood by the "usual examination on Friday morning" being mentioned now and then.

CHAPTER 3

A Log Book shows Life in School

Now, a closer look at Chale's earliest log book[40] to help understand the life the children led. Dating from the summer of 1869 until January 1873, and covering parts of both Abraham Baker's and James Bryant's mastership, the book illustrates much of the findings of the Newcastle Commission.

School hours are not mentioned, but judging from later records, children arrived about 9 o'clock, and lessons finished at 4. There was a brief playtime at mid-morning and afternoon. Lunch - or rather dinner-time - was somewhere between 12 noon and 2 o'clock, lasting for longer than is usual nowadays to allow most of the children to walk home to join their parents for the main meal of the day. Those from the more distant areas (Atherfield is 3 miles from the school, and other houses in the parish are 2 miles away) would bring whatever food was available, maybe just a wedge of bread.

Attendance, and its great concern to the staff, has already been mentioned (see page 13). The log book shows just how apparently careless both children and parents were. Every week the average was recorded, sometimes with glee "Attendance to-day is higher than it has been at any time before, morning 89, evening 90". At other times "The whole school (was) exhorted to attend regularly and punctually". In between comes "fair attendance", "attendance thin to-day" or "several children absent without leave". Some scolding creeps in as "Harriet Godden and Sophia Hookey very irregular in attendance" and "several children absent without leave - Master spoken about before the whole school", "Parents are very indifferent in the matter".

Farming needs were put before schooling when it came to the busy times of haymaking and harvest, not unusual in rural areas across the country. Chale children were expected to help in the fields, and to some extent the teachers were resigned to this. So they recorded "Haymaking has thinned the school children", "A few away because of harvest", and (almost with a sigh of relief) "Broke up for harvest holidays for 5 weeks". Even after that there was the gleaning. One year this went on into October, "gleaning still remains unfinished" and that meant a "thin attendance".

The weather, of course, was another influence. On 14 June 1869 "Many absent because rain a.m. - but could have come p.m. and didn't". Three days later it was very wet again, "...children from afar came while near ones didn't". Cold, wet winters and muddy, rough and stony lanes kept many from school. It was not unusual to read as in January 1873 "A very poor attendance indeed...The great reason given being that they had no boots to wear". Poverty was such that many went barefoot, keeping what footwear they had for Sunday best, and always "boots" never shoes. Even in the late twentieth century local lanes flood, and a hundred years earlier children had no mackintoshes or wellingtons, and there were no buses or cars to transport them.

Children were absent for many reasons. Epidemics of scarlatina, whooping cough, measles and so on swept through the school, as did the usual coughs and colds. The illness of a mother frequently meant a girl had to stay at home to care for the rest of the family.

A multitude of other excuses for non-appearance were also recorded. Some played truant and were "punished", reading between the lines this meant the cane. This was the fate of Frank Coombs, George and Fanny Bull, Walter Woodford and many others. Two of the boys followed the hounds one day, but as they were canny enough to "beg Master's pardon" and as it was "a rare occurance (sic)" they were not severely punished. William Morris also stayed away without leave for 1½ days, but his aunt punished him so he got off with a caution "not to repeat the offence".

Other pleas of absence reflected Chale's seafaring interests. June is the time when shoals of mackerel arrive off-shore and in 1870 "Some few children are absent to see mackrel (sic) caught". Several were away in October, too, "owing to the Sale of the remains of the wrecked Brig". Some reasons given are more tenuous - "Easter Monday I suppose is keeping a few away", (this before that day was a regular Bank Holiday); the false report of a holiday; and "the least appearance of rain the greater part of the children absent themselves".

Again and again a note of desperation occurs as particular offenders are mentioned. "Charles Orchard attends very irregularly of late and never asks leave". Children were sometimes taken off the register for non-attendance. In April 1872, George and John Grimstone from Atherfield "readmitted again this week their parents promising to send them more regular than hitherto". Some scholars, according to the book, made it a practice to stay away part of every week.

The chance of work also kept children away. Kate Sprake could only attend as a half-timer, from May 1871, as she had to work in the mornings for the Rector's wife. Part-time schooling was common and acceptable, particularly for the older children. Henry Jenkins was given three weeks leave so he could stand-in as groom to a local gentleman. Another boy, Daniel King, was absent "having gone to work for a few weeks". This was in mid-summer, so it is likely he was helping on a farm.

This irregularity has to be understood not purely as indifference to education, but associated with trying to change the centuries old cultural and traditional ways of living. The family had long been an economic unit, and children's work made a valuable contribution. Their education had consisted of learning their gender role in the home from their parents. The idea of some Authority, whether Church, State or Teacher, requiring boys and girls to absent themselves from home for about 6 hours a day to learn something totally unconnected (as the parents saw it) with earning a living just didn't sink in. In isolated farming districts, such as Chale, the seasons and the weather were more important than clock-time.

One event in these early years that brought nearly everyone to school was the distribution of the Bread at Christmas time. This was part of Sir Henry Worsley's gift (see page 7), but the log writer seems ignorant of this merely recording "24 Dec. 1869. This afternoon in accordance with request[ix] of some benevolent gentleman loaves of Bread were distributed among the children in the Upper Schools. Most fameleys (sic) getting two gallons[x]."

The curriculum followed the instructions given by Messrs Weekes and Barber. Reading, writing and arithmetic were emphasised. Sometimes the reading is said to be "improving", or "making some improvement", though also "I am not at all satisfied with the reading" appeared. Often the Rector came to hear the children and give a lesson, this must have been a great help to the headmaster, who can't have found it easy to listen to all 50 or so pupils in his charge.
    Along with reading went regular dictation (which, of course, took in writing), and spelling. There seemed to be much trouble over both. "Mary Thorn very careless with her spelling and dictation"; "Several found not able to spell the word 'against'"; and in November 1872 "Spelling seems to be the weakest subject". It is sad to relate, but very much a sign of the attitude to teaching and learning that a boy was punished with the cane for mistakes in spelling. It seems all the more unreasonable since the log writer (Martha Brown - more of her later) was herself a poor speller. She was confused by the "i before e" rule, put double "t's" where there should be single ones, and vice versa, had problems with apostrophes, and made many other errors.
    As for arithmetic, a childish verse of the era went like this:

> "Multiplication is vexation
> Division is as bad
> The rule of three doth puzzle me
> And fractions drive me mad.
>   (Anon. Quote by man born 1879)

This appears to have been the feeling of Chale school children. Almost every week the log book reports difficulties with the subject. So in July 1869 the second class "do not seem to improve very fast". A few weeks later came "The first class require practice in the Compound rules of Money". The master taught "Standard IV Long Division, very little knowledge shown". Another time he spent "nearly all week on multiplication by two figures". Martha Brown's plaintive comment on one occasion was "The arithmetic of Standard III was not so well done as it ought (to be) considering the time spent with this Standard by Master". She did not take into

---

[ix] Probably should have read "bequest"
[x] A gallon loaf = about 4 Kg or just over 8 lbs

account that perhaps the method and/or standard of teaching was poor, and the subject anyway beyond the comprehension of extremely unsophisticated country children.

Scripture, in accordance with the National Society's rules, was regularly, even frequently taught, often by the Rector. From the Infant Class on the children had to learn the Lord's Prayer, Creed, Catechism and 10 Commandments by heart. Study also included "the Structure and contents of the Tabernacle made by Moses" (which covers about 6 chapters in the Old Testament Book of Exodus), the Book of Judges, and the "deliverance by Gideon". Much of this may have been over the children's heads as "some of the second class extremely dull in Scripture", and an abstract on the lesson dealing with the healing of the man with a withered hand was "very inferior". Two or three times a term the children went to Church for a half hour service, and always on special festival days. The 1st and 2nd class went occasionally to "practice with the organ", knowledge of hymns and other Church music being important.

Again in accordance with the bequests, the girls were taught sewing. They had to present a piece of needlework when Her Majesty's Inspector visited and one child, Kate Sprake, neglected to finish hers at home and was severely reprimanded. Sewing can't have been a very popular subject as the Rector's wife found fault with it on one occasion, and in June 1871 "Several girls punished to-day for not doing their work properly in sewing lesson". Besides their regular lesson the girls (and sometimes the boys) attended Dorcas meetings held in the school. The Dorcas Society was a Christian Charitable organisation for ladies who met together to sew clothes for the poor. Chale's Society made garments on behalf of the Ragged Schools in London. These meetings caused some disruption, and probably a welcome change from routine. Classrooms had to be rearranged and pupils were moved from their usual places. At one there were "20 boys and girls present with Ladies from neighbourhood".

Geography and Music are referred to but only in a small way. "The usual geography lesson", "..abstract of geography very fairly done by upper standards". As for music, the children learnt new chants for the Te Deum, and various singing pieces with such titles as "Oh Call my brother back to me" and "If I were a Sunbeam".

Certainly this school was run, as laid down by the National Society, on the 'monitorial' system. With numbers averaging between 60 and 80 and only the Master, an assistant, and someone for the infants, teaching cannot have been easy, especially in those small schoolrooms. June 1869 records that children were taken in turn from 1st and 2nd classes to teach 3rd and 4th classes[xi]. One entry mentions "Sebastian Bastiani and Robert Sprake monitors this week". A week later Robert is praised because he "keeps good order with his class". This contrasts with Henry Jenkins, Monitor, who "does not keep such order as I should like". Later that same year there is a plaintive note from the headteacher "I find the want of a Pupil Teacher or good Monitor".

[xi] This seems odd, possibly should have been the other way i.e. 3rd & 4th teach 1st & 2nd.

That master left the next summer, and a new one, Mr James Bryant, took over in September 1870. He also found the job a taxing one. In the May following his appointment Martha Brown wrote "Master finds the want of assistance"

Punishment always loomed for the wrong-doer, for misbehaviour in Church, for neglecting to learn verses (this boy besides being punished "on the hand" was kept in, but showed enough spirit to run out of school as soon as the master left). The list goes on, for "refusing to do as he was bid", "for telling an untruth" and "for copying". Now that corporal punishment in schools is banned, it seems incredible that caning was once a daily occurrence, and accepted as necessary even by humane people. Some of the parents tried to stand up for their children. Those of Clara Chiverton, who had been punished for truancy, "treated (the Master) with very threatening language". When Clara and her sister next went to school they were sent home with a note that they could not be readmitted until the mother had seen the rector and the school managers. The same was required of the mothers of Charles Orchard and Rose Hendy.

A strange entry in 1869 states "Log not kept because didn't know if School was to come under Government Inspection (awaiting decision of Committee of Council)". The question was resolved by June and the log was then resumed. The coming of Her Majesty's Inspector was very important to the teachers (as it still is), and obviously created nervousness, not surprising when a school's grant depended upon his report. From the time when the Rector received notice of HMI's visit until the named day arrived, tension mounted. Attendance was crucial, in some cases mothers were persuaded to bring sick children, just so heads could be counted. A few days prior to the visit (in April 1871) the children were "informed of the Inspection and exhorted to be present".

It may sound as if school life was hard, and so it was compared to today, but the odd one day holiday lightened it. Coronation day, a holiday which appears to have been unique to the Isle of Wight, was celebrated at the end of June. Probably instituted during Queen Victoria's residence at Osborne House, it is now forgotten though it continued until the Second World War. Half-holidays were frequent, and given for all sorts of reasons - a Teachers' Conference; to give time to prepare room for "Penny Readings" in the evening; on Ascension Day; and when the Master had to go and lead the singing at a Church in another parish. The children had "treats", too, when various "teas" were arranged by the rector, the schoolmaster or the local gentry.

In the late nineteenth century it was obvious that Chale's school was the focus of much attention in the community. It must have created some divided loyalty among the pupils, however. Were they to obey Authority and attend regularly? Or go to work at the instigation of parents and parents' employers? And as far as parents were concerned, they could not see why, respected as they usually were, the schoolmaster and the rector should have such a say in the up-bringing of their children.

A Particularly Happy Little School

On the national scene the Education Act of 1870 became law, and brought changes and an important compromise which went some way to solving the "religious difficulty". In addition the state's involvement in education was strengthened, and compulsory schooling came a step nearer.

20

CHAPTER 4

The "Conscience Clause" & so on

This very significant Act, spanned by Chale's first available log book, had far-reaching effects on schooling. In remote areas, however, many village schools were still firmly in the hands of the Church of England and few changes were immediately evident.

By this time education was being demanded in the expanding populations and spreading conurbations of England. Working class parents were beginning to see the advantages of reading and writing. Others saw it as a means of controlling the growing army of unruly children. Churches felt that being able to read the Bible would ensure the raising of good Christians. The courts hoped it would control a wave of crime that the increased population brought. And employers of the Industrial Revolution found they needed literate workers to cope with new jobs being created. It became impossible for either premises or staff to be provided by voluntary organisations. The onus, therefore, fell upon the state at least to provide buildings and the Education Department was given the duty of finding out where school accommodation was required. The Department also had to make arrangements for School Boards to be set up in each district (i.e. parish or municipal borough) to make provision where needed. Officially to be named Public Elementary Schools, these were often called Board Schools or Provided Schools, and fees for instruction were not to exceed 9d (about 3½p) per week.

The most notable item of the 1870 Act (in view of the on-going conflict between state and various churches) was, however, the inclusion of the "conscience" or Cowper-Temple clause (after its author)[41]. Parents of pupils at these new schools were given the option of withdrawing their children from religious instruction. Such teaching was to take place either at the beginning or the end of the day, so children either came later or left earlier in order to avoid the lessons (hence 'morning assembly'). A notice giving the timetable was to be exhibited in the classroom. These pupils were also allowed leave of absence on days of special religious observance in their own church or chapel.

While the scriptures could still be studied, all instruction had to be non-denominational, only doctrine common to all Christian people (e.g. the Lord's Prayer) was to be taught. In fact this was what had been advocated many years before by Joseph Lancaster, the founder of the British and Foreign Schools Society.

One other stipulation concerning the conscience clause was that in Board Schools, though Her Majesty's Inspectors (HMIs) had powers to visit them at any time, they did not have authority to inquire into religious teaching. There was also to be no Parliamentary Grant in respect of such lessons.

Finance for building the new schools was to come from the rates. This left the Voluntary (or Non-Provided) Schools in the position of being state-aided (by annual capitation grants) under private management, but not rate-supported. They were offered the option of transferring their schools to the local School Board, but this meant losing autonomy and the necessity of agreeing to the conscience clause. Consequently many voluntary schools remained under the jurisdiction of their founders, as in Chale. It also put rate-payers who subscribed to a Voluntary School in the position of subsidising a type of education (i.e. Board School building) they perhaps did not agree with. This, of course, did nothing to soothe the antagonism between the voluntary and the state "provided" schools.

In addition the 1870 Act made a move towards free and compulsory education. The School Boards were empowered to reimburse the fees of children whose parents could not afford to pay, and were allowed to make their own bye-laws on the matter of attendance. From the time of its Charity School status, Chale had accepted non-paying pupils (see page 5). In July 1871 notices were sent out for all Chale children "to pay their pence quarterly in advance". Within a few days most of the children "in the Master's room" paid their one shilling (5p) for the coming quarter (i.e. one old penny per week). In the same year the log book records fees of two pence per week for a newly admitted pupil, William Stephens from Atherfield Coastguard Station. A sliding scale, therefore, seems to have been in operation, and may have indicated the relative affluence of families in government employment.

It was expected, but not enforced, that children over 5 and up to 13 years went to school. Bye-laws could be made, however, exempting a child, or allowing him or her to leave sooner under certain conditions as follows:

(1)   the child to have reached a standard of education required by HMI:

(2)   there to be proof that the child was receiving instruction in an efficient manner elsewhere;

(3)   sickness or other unavoidable cause prevented further attendance; and

(4)   there was no public elementary school within three miles of the child's home.

No record of a Chale child qualifying to leave under condition 1 has been found. Some children did start work before age 13, "receiving instruction" probably being interpreted as learning a trade or calling. Sometimes this was temporary as Henry Jenkins' case (see page 16), or at haymaking or harvest. The "unavoidable cause" may refer to a girl having to take care of the family should the mother die or have to go out to work. This happened to Janet Squibb who was kept at home while her mother "went out to look after Mr W H Jacobs". A child's sickness or some sort of disability undoubtedly occurred from time to time. Amelia Gordon was admitted aged 7½ years in April 1891, but left through illness, and was re-admitted a year later.

How accurately the 3 miles from home was measured is not known, but the Atherfield Coastguard Cottages were certainly on the borderline.

This latitude regarding school attendance continued until 1876 when another Act made school attendance compulsory, though the exceptions above could still apply. A Committee was set up at the same time to enforce the ruling.

Through Chale's early log book and matters under discussion in Parliamentary circles, much is revealed of the functioning of the community at the time. The school became the local centre for social and official gatherings, bringing in many people who were not parents. The Vestry Meeting (similar to to-day's Parish Council) moved their venue as early as 1847 from the Church to the "Parochial Schools of the Parish of Chale"[42]. As already mentioned, the local ladies of the Dorcas Society met in school for their sewing afternoons. The "Treats" reported in the log book were held in school, too. "Mrs Barton kindly promised to give Choir Children a tea on Thursday evening" was an entry for January 1870, and two years later all the children were given tea by "Mrs Roach and Lady friends at 4.30". It is hardly likely that the ladies would have appreciated some 80 rural school children in heavy boots in their homes.

In the absence of village halls (a great many of which were built after the First World War) the local school was used for many public (and private) gatherings. Formerly the church or the inn had served as a meeting place - but the former was cold, and the latter was suspected of leading to all sorts of temptations, and anyway was not considered a proper place for women. Some communities had a Parish Room, Chale's was part of the large Georgian Rectory half a mile from the school. These were all very well for church occasions, but were not available for secular events, and as part of the rector's home Chale's was unsuitable.

Another way in which the school was becoming integrated into the village was through the many roles of the head teacher. In the days of charity schools the rector and churchwardens often made the appointment, the master or mistress being answerable to them in all respects, and relying on their goodwill to remain in post. Advantage was often taken of this and various other tasks were put upon the teacher, so that sometimes he or she led a very busy life. Little is known of Chale's early headteachers, but certainly by the late nineteenth century they were much involved in parish life.

Mr James Bryant, who was appointed Chale schoolmaster in 1870, was elected Assistant Overseer of the Parish in September of that year. The minutes of the Vestry Meeting report that he was told "his duties would include the collection of all Rates and Taxes, and the transacting of all other Parish business hitherto devolving on the assistant Overseer of the Parish..." to which he agreed[43]. Over the ensuing years Mr Bryant was instructed to "request payment" of various overdue rates, rents and taxes. His successors, Henry Flint (1879), George Amos (1882) and John Cooke (1891), followed him in the post, all at the same salary - £30 per annum. Mr Amos asked for an increase in 1885, apparently to the astonishment of the Vestry Meeting.

After a brief discussion they decided to consider the request at the next meeting...and that was all that was recorded of it[44]. Mr Cooke received the same amount until changes in local government at the end of the century brought a different system of rate collection.

Many schoolmasters, including Chale's, were expected to help with the choir. (How unfortunate for the applicant with no ear for music.) Mr Bryant gave the children a holiday on 8 November 1871 because a neighbouring Church was "reopened on that day...Master having occasion to go and lead the singing". Again on Good Friday (usually an ordinary working day) school was closed as "Master" had to attend Church twice.

While it is not actually recorded that Mr Amos filled the role, he was very much involved in writing songs. Chale school children performed some of these at their concerts, others were sold to "well known composers and publishers" (according to a local newspaper account)[45]. Such obvious aptitude must surely have been put to use in Church. Mr Cooke trained and led the Church choir into the twentieth century, and is well remembered in that capacity by many elderly residents to-day.

Besides teaching and song-writing Mr Amos had contributed plays and dialogues to leading education journals of the time, and he was also a successful fiction writer[46]. Such a talented man was, however, unlikely to remain in the static situation a village school offered. In August 1891 he moved on to become headmaster of a large National school for boys in Bristol. His last service to Chale was as the "able and indefatigable hon. secretary" of the committee which organised the Chale and Niton Athletic Sports that summer[47]. His leadership had been very successful and the local paper reported that in his time "Chale school has been raised to a leading position in the Island". On his departure grateful parishioners gave him a gold watch inscribed "Presented to Mr G Amos in recognition of 9 years' faithful service". His successor, John Cooke, was also secretary to the sports committee. Photographs in the hands of local families confirm that early in the next century he was to become Scout Master of Chale's newly formed troop.

By 1870 there were between 70 and 90 children at Chale school. The numbers fluctuated with the comings and goings of the coastguards and their families, and the annual movement of agricultural labourers in the autumn. An admissions register for the years 1870 to 1893 survives and supplies further information about both children and parents, and about the staff making the entries[48].

Martha Brown's spelling let her down again (as in the log book), so Mabel appears as Mable, Reginald is Regniald, and Louisa is Lousia, not once but several times. Addresses given are very vague (just the name of the hamlet e.g. Pyle or Corve), and this makes it difficult to decide whether children of the same surname are brothers and sisters, or cousins. While this looks like carelessness, it may mean the writer **knew** where everyone lived, or reflect the fact that the school was run by only one qualified master with one unqualified assistant and the work-load was excessive.

24

What is remarkable is the very early age at which the children were still being admitted (see page 5). Most were under 5 and many only 3 years old. The extension to the school in 1857 was specifically for an Infant Room, and obviously good use was being made of it. All the Browns, "Regniald", Bertha, William and Maurice, started school in various years between these dates, when each reached the age of 3 years and 3 months old. Their father was the local grocer, and they lived at Chale Green about a mile from the school. John Bull was under 4 in 1876, and he had to walk nearly 2 miles from Walpen, and, of course, home again. Two families of Chivertons (15 of them being admitted between 1875 and 1890) lived near each other at Blackgang and trudged about the same distance, presumably the older ones helped the young ones along.

Another aspect of residents' lives is revealed in the occupations followed by the parents. The majority simply called themselves "labourers", 57 fathers go by this label. Some worked full-time on farms as stockmen or general agricultural workers, others would have been casually employed either on farm, building, road or other work. During the winter when extra help was not required on farms and building work practically ceased, with no social services provision, feeding the family must have been a nightmare.

Others whose work was associated with agriculture were listed as hurdlemaker, thatcher, shepherds, three blacksmiths and several dairymen and farmers. Three sawyers were recorded, reminding present day residents that there used to be a sawpit on the Green. Domestic needs were catered for by grocers (2), bakers (3), shoemaker (1) and a brewer. A policeman was mentioned in Chale from 1884. A hawker was also listed, presumably an itinerant pedlar.

After farming the next most common occupation was coastguard, and over this period 48 men moved to and away from Chale in this service. Also associated with the sea were 5 full-time fishermen, one sailor and a diver.

It is sad to say that 17 families were marked as fatherless, and the memory of fishermen drowned continues to be strong in the village where descendants still live. Loss of the man of the family, whether at sea or by accident or illness, must have resulted in extremes of poverty, contributing to the lack of boots, and need for the Christmas hand-out of bread.

In the wider world various less momentous Education Acts had been passed. In 1880 a short Act re-inforced compulsory schooling, and School Boards were ordered to frame bye-laws regarding attendance. In 1887 another Royal Commission was set up, to enquire into the working of the Act passed in 1876. Following the report of this commission, free education came in with a Parliamentary grant being made in lieu of fees (i.e. the Fee Grant). At the same time (1891) many of the commissioners were in favour of rate-aid being given to voluntary schools. This, however, was not to be implemented for another decade, when radical changes in the education system took place. The Voluntary Schools Act was passed in 1897, giving special grant aid of 5 shillings (25p) per head in average attendance to denominational schools[49].

Difficulties were being experienced at Chale in 1888, '89 and '90 when the school's accounts show £18, £26 and £43 respectively "advanced by the Treasurer" (i.e. the rector, Rev. C.W.Heald) to balance the books[50]. The list of donors and subscribers is given, more than half the amounts being one guinea or less, the highest (from the rector) was £7, and the total was £66.11.6d. The endowment brought in £19.10s, and the government grant came to a little more than the subscriptions. Repeatedly between 1882 and 1890 a debit balance was recorded.

The account was still in deficit for the year 1901-02, when the school was £47.7s.11d overdrawn at the bank. The next year this was reduced to about £35, but donations were well down. By this time Chale was receiving three grants - Aid Grant, Annual Grant and Fee Grant.

At the bottom of each set of accounts appears a summary of HMI's report for the year. The 1882 comments were mediocre, there was a "falling off in Writing and Spelling. Grammar and Geography seem hardly to have been taught above the Second Standard". However, discipline seems to have been satisfactory, there had been an increase in numbers so more desks were needed, and the Infants' Needlework was said to be "particularly good". Mr Amos took over the school in that year, and his success is evident by 1888 when "Discipline deserves praise. The elementary subjects are good, decided improvement has been effected. English and Geography are fair. Needlework is well taught". In the Infants' class "The instruction of the Infants deserves much praise". Similar comments are also added to the other account sheets[51].

Before the end of the century Chale school was involved in more expense for extensions and improvements to the building. Perhaps the new headteacher, John Cooke, who arrived in 1891 and was to be in charge for the next 30 years, instigated the work. In 1893 Messrs G W & E Creeth of Niton quoted £128 for "alterations and additions to the Schools and offices". The plans and specifications are not available, but the detailed invoice and statement of accounts show that the total, including materials, builders' account, architect's fees and various other small amounts, came to nearly £220[52]. A large entrance lobby with pegs for coats was added, a new path with steps, and a coke shed constructed, and the exterior painted. Many small repairs and improvements were done such as mending the stove pipe and putting up book shelves, repairs to windows, fitting blinds, improving toilet facilities (by all accounts these remained primitive for another half century). One's heart goes out to F Weeks and H Chiverton who dug sand for 3 and 4 days respectively at a wage of 3 shillings (30p) per day, all meticulously detailed in the accounts.

Paying for all this once again fell mainly on kindly patrons, and the generosity of local residents. Some years before, Chale school had received a legacy from a lady named Blackford which had been invested in Consols[53]. This was now "called in" and yielded £63.11s.8d. The Nutter family put on a concert that raised £5.10s., other grants and donations came from as far afield as Staffordshire (the late Mrs Moseley of Leaton Hall gave £10). Some contributions were in kind - stone from Lady Mary Gordon (who owned land in the parish), lime from Mr Way of Pyle, and sand from Mr C Dabell of Blackgang. Yet others provided "cartage" (presumably sending their workers with horse and wagon to move stone etc), including Messrs. Jolliffe, Way, Morris, Russell, Spanner and Sprake (all local residents). There was still a shortfall, however, and once again the National Society was approached and came to the rescue with £15[54].

In his letter of application to the latter (dated 18 Jan. 1894) the Reverend C W Heald adds a sentence which confirms the "religious problem" in Chale. He says "We have had the misfortune to lose £5.16.6 a year subscriptions which were those of dissenters"(his emphasis). And on the application form itself in answer to a question re "peculiar local difficulties" he wrote "This is a poor agricultural Parish. There is a strong dissenting element and recently we have lost some good subscriptions owing to our refusal to discontinue teaching the Church Catechism"[55].

This community effort, as in many villages, had improved the building, and no doubt made working conditions for both pupils and staff more comfortable. The thought of 80 wet coats in the classroom daily over much of the winter is not very edifying, and the steamy atmosphere produced in conjunction with the coke stove cannot have been very healthy. It was to be another 60 years before there were further major alterations, though, of course, over those years the building gradually gained smaller twentieth century amenities.

But what a century the nineteenth had been, certainly for England, and in no small way for the education of Chale children. Since the 1841 census, though Chale's daily life had hardly changed, the population had almost doubled from 353 in 1788 to 607 in 1891[56]. The sea and the land were still the main providers of work for large close-knit families. Victorian prosperity, solidarity and paternalism apparently continued to hold the village community together. The relationship between Church and Chapel was the largest difficulty in this one small parish. Throughout the Isle of Wight strong non-conformist support existed which undermined the traditional authority of the Church of England.

In many ways, however, outside influences hardly reached the village. Neither the Napoleonic, the Crimean, nor the Boer wars seem to have made any great impression on the inhabitants. One monument within the parish remembers the first two of these conflicts. High on St Catherine's Down stands a pillar commemorating on the north side the visit to England of the Tsar of Russia in 1814 (at the end of the Napoleonic Wars), and on the south the men who fell at Sebastopol. The idyll was nevertheless coming to an end, and from the second year of the new century enormous (and not entirely welcome) educational changes occurred, soon to be followed by the horrors of the First World War, and the many other events that have re-shaped both schooling and whole communities over the past 100 years.

CHAPTER 5

Changes Galore

The Education Act of 1902 brought these new challenges, and Chale obediently put into practice the many requirements. The Appointed Day for changeover was set for the Autumn of the following year. John Cooke's first entry in his new Log Book (called No.1) read "October 1st 1903. Schools taken over by the County Council, under the new Education Act." A bald statement, perhaps, but one that hid sadness that the school was losing autonomy, trepidation concerning the outcome, and outrage over the circumstances that had brought this about. A more positive response was relief that the provision of rate aid would lift financial burdens. The state had, however, intervened to such an extent through this Act that the Church's influence on the education of the poor was never to be so strong again.

Over the years of its evolution, elementary school education had become fragmented, there were varying standards, and differing influences, poor children were being offered a very unco-ordinated system. The aim of the Act was to draw up a frame-work so that all pupils began life with a similar background of opportunity to learn. So much needed doing - building construction, teacher training, the curriculum extended and standardised, and beyond that the provision of secondary education, arts, science and technical training, plus changes at University level. The first decade of the twentieth century saw an immense amount of innovation, progress and improvement throughout the educational system, much of it beyond the scope of this book. Elementary education at village school level is the concern here.

The Act of 1902 has been referred to as "the veritable charter of incorporation of English education"[67]. It brought voluntary (Non-Provided) schools (formerly relying on private subscriptions plus Government grant) and Board (Provided) schools (financed through rate-aid in addition to grants) on to a more equal footing. Both religious and secular influences in school management came together when all schools were taken over by Local Education Authorities (LEAs) set up by each county or county borough. There was no actual compulsion upon the small Parochial Schools (the designation "Church of England Schools" began in 1907)[68] to come under the new authority, but it was clear that private donations could not compete with funds available under the LEA. As already pointed out, many village schools were finding increasing difficulty in meeting expenses, let alone expanding into the needs of the twentieth century. The deal offered to them, though a compromise, certainly seemed to provide the means of continuing their aim of raising children in the ways of the Established Church, while relieving them of their constant money worries.

Briefly the main provisions were:

1. The LEA was to have control over all secular instruction.
2. Voluntary schools were to have Managers, consisting of four "Foundation" managers, i.e. chosen by those formerly in full control of the school (C of E schools usually had the parish priest, plus the churchwardens or other respected residents) and two others (one appointed by the LEA and the other by a minor local authority, e.g. the Parish Council).
3. (a) The LEA to maintain and keep the schools efficient. To this end the managers had to carry out the LEA's directives regarding secular instruction; and the appointment or dismissal of teachers was to be approved by the LEA, though with some latitude. Consent to appointment could only be withheld on educational grounds, and no consent was required for dismissal if this was connected with giving of religious instruction.
(b) The managers had to provide the school premises for use as a public elementary school with no fees to be charged. They also had to keep the buildings in good repair, and if necessary bring them up to a standard that might reasonably be required by the authority.
(c) Assistant teachers or pupil-teachers could be appointed without reference to their religious denomination, and the LEA could make the final choice if there were several candidates for one post.

These arrangements brought both advantages and disadvantages to the voluntary schools. Many church people were of the opinion that all their work in education was being denigrated. One Chale resident said (somewhat ungrammatically and erroneously but illustrating the depth of the ordinary person's feelings) "It was all forgotten what these good ministers and churchmen had done. It was tried to rob the church of her schools and the endowments which had been given them.[59] And indeed a clause directing that income from educational endowments should be paid to the authority for the relief of parochial rates, was included. Chale, however, managed to retain its Charities, but not without a struggle.

The Rector (Rev. C W Heald) brought the matter up with the National Society as early as February, 1903[60]. He wrote a letter setting out the position and asking "whether...we ought to seek an interview with the Local Education Authority...". The reply does not survive, but he wrote again in September requesting advice urgently. He was told "you should write...and say that in your opinion a part of the Endowment should be allowed towards the expenses of the Sunday School, as on that day as well as on the week day it will be the duty of a schoolmaster to teach the Catechism". Whatever was done was effective as an Order dated April 1905, set out the way in which Chale's Charities were to be used[61]. Many years later they were still being distributed in accordance with this Order, that is for general educational use rather than as part of the headteacher's salary.

Some non-conformist ratepayers refused to pay that part of their rates earmarked for education. They were now compelled to send their children to school, even if the only one available happened to be C. of E. (or other denomination different from their own). The Cowper-Temple clause had had to be accepted by voluntary schools in order to receive rate aid. Nevertheless, widespread opposition resulted in a campaign for non-payment, which was named "Passive Resistance" (perhaps the first instance of the expression). In some areas, particularly in Wales, the Board of Education had to take steps to assist schools whose funds were much depleted by this action.

Chale was involved in a small way. The Rector sent another letter to the National Society, in 1904, with two complaints[62]. A member of the education committee who happened to live locally, had visited the school during a religious lesson. Mr Heald said "I suppose he considers that he has a right to meddle with the religious instruction. He is not even a representative manager. He is a 'passive resister'; and of course a strong opponent to the Church teaching". His other problem was with the LEA Manager, a lady preacher and "a bitter enemy of the Church...she considers the Catechism to be 'deadly' teaching'", who wished to sit in on a religious lesson. She apparently wanted to check that all the "Bible lessons" were non-denominational. Mr Heald sought corroboration that teaching in a Church school still remained Church of England biased. He also wanted to know whether he had the power to prohibit such visits. He ends his letter "I have earnestly endeavoured to avoid strife or unpleasantness with non-conformists". He served the village until 1927 and is still remembered for his kindness to everyone whatever their religious conviction.

The Rev. Heald had yet more queries, he wrote again in the same year asking whether the LEA could insist that he alter the timetable to start morning prayers ten minutes earlier[63]. He felt this would result in inconvenience and possibly much interruption of the lesson. The National Society informed him that the LEA could not "interfere with reasonable facilities for religious instruction during school hours".

As time went on these controversies quietened down. However, if so much dissatisfaction was experienced in one small, isolated village school on the remote Isle of Wight it surely indicated that feelings were running very high throughout the country. Nearly a hundred years later the problems seem trivial and the fuss is difficult to understand as attitudes have changed so much, but at the time the "religious question" loomed large (see page 4), and there was heartache in many parishes. Non-conformist children had long attended Chale school, and the first evidence of withdrawal from religious instruction appears in the Admissions Book for 1907, when 5 year old Fanny Parker was exempted.

Gradually other areas of the Act were implemented. Chale's school buildings were inspected, as were those of all voluntary schools. By this time the Infants were using the former boys' schoolroom on the south of the headmaster's house. Older children were all in the large classroom now called the "Mixed School" which had a partition to provide a smaller area when needed. The required space per pupil (9 sq.ft. for Infants, 10 sq. ft. for Mixed School) was adequately met. In other ways, however, the buildings did not come up to standard.

The inspection, carried out soon after the 1902 Act, reported flooring, glazing and furniture required repair. Interior decoration needed doing, locks and fastenings put in working order and cloakroom pegs renewed. The heating throughout was said to be poor. The stove in the Infants' room was in "a very dilapidated condition", and anyway was not suitable for keeping the room warm enough for infants. A system of heating by hot water was suggested, but this was never followed up, possibly it was too expensive, especially as the school would have had to pay (see page 29 [b]).

The ventilation apparently was totally unacceptable. The inspector, Mr Blizard, wanted ventilators fitted capable of changing the air three times an hour. Though he does allow that the wind being very strong in winter in Chale this type of ventilation might make the rooms too cold. The windows provided just about enough daylight, and artificial light, he reported, was by oil lamps.

The toilets, referred to as "offices", consisted of earth closets, 3 for boys, 5 for girls one of which was reserved for the headmaster's household. Properly maintained these were acceptable, but a boys' urinal that had no water supply and drained directly into a ditch, thence under the playground and eventually out to sea, was not. The water supply came from the public provision in Chale, that is from a reservoir on Batt's Hill, towards St Catherine's Down. One tap was laid on to a basin in the hat and coat area and a second to the master's scullery. The Inspector did not think any of this suitable or adequate. However, reading details of facilities at other Island schools, Chale's seem to have been among the better buildings. The offices of a school in a neighbouring village were totally unhygienic, and loathsome in the extreme.

The Inspector's final remarks concerned the playground. He said there should be a division between boys' and girls' playground, and that it should be paved, gravelled and drained. Once all the above works were done he came to the conclusion that the school would be "well adapted for elementary teaching" ... Except that he also required a cloakroom built for Infants and Girls, and a small larder to hold the children's dinners.

Were these recommendations carried out? They must have been for the school to be accepted by the LEA - or a compromise reached. No record has been found but such work would have meant further expense for the school managers (see page 29 [b]).

The teaching staff's qualifications were looked into. Mr and Mrs Cooke, who had been Headteacher and Assistant for over 10 years, were "certificated", so their continued employment was not in doubt. Precise details of their training are not available, but it is probable that they attended one of the "Voluntary" Colleges (a Church of England one in this case).

As early as the 1840s James Kay (later Sir James Kay-Shuttleworth) had begun the movement to replace monitors by a pupil-teacher system, and provide facilities for the best pupil-teachers to continue training. To this end he founded residential colleges, the first, St John's College, Battersea, was later taken over by the National Society. Many establishments run on similar lines followed, and soon the Church had training colleges in most diocese, and other denominations set up their own. These "voluntary" colleges became important for the training of teachers for the elementary school system, and by the beginning of the twentieth century courses had been standardised and lasted two years. They were all denominational, with no "conscience clause" to allow students of other faiths to attend.

By 1893 the training monopoly of the above colleges was broken, when the Universities were allowed to offer grant-aided training for elementary school teachers[64]. Further advances were made with the 1902 Act, when LEAs were empowered to found and maintain training colleges, for which building grants were given 3 years later. These had no religious affiliation, and they were often for day attendance only.

The Act also made it possible for LEAs to establish secondary schools. Following this, they could require entrants to colleges to have had 4 years secondary education. This greatly helped to widen the teachers' outlook. As pupil-teachers, some young people had formerly gained their only experience in the elementary system, even spent a lifetime in the same school. Through these reforms came the gradual disappearance of pupil-teachers, except in rural areas.

One of those who was a pupil and then carried on as a pupil-teacher at Chale was Miss Martha Brown, the early log keeper at the school. Soon after the Appointed Day, in October 1903, Mr Cooke recorded "Miss Brown, the Infant Mistress, having resigned, by request of the Old Managers, Mrs Cooke, the Certificated Assistant, had been temporally (sic) transferred to take charge of the Infants Dept. from Sept.14...". Another simple statement that must hide much heartache and sadness. Miss Brown had taught there for over 50 years, starting at 14 years old, but never having the opportunity of attending college. So when everything changed, was updated and became impersonal, she having reached retirement age, had to go.

She lived in a tiny cottage just across the road from the school, and knew everyone. Teaching had been her life. She died just over a year later, on 31 December 1904 aged 65. Perhaps being asked to leave broke her heart. An apt text from Isaiah is inscribed on her tombstone in Chale Churchyard "And all the children shall be taught of the Lord and great shall be the peace of thy children". Even in those far off days educational reorganisation meant the agony of redundancies and compulsory retirements.

Following Miss Brown's departure, two sisters, the Misses Arabella and Julia Sprake, assisted Mrs Cooke. Neither of them was trained, so they were among those last pupil-teachers found in rural areas. Miss Arabella (who had taught at the school since the mid-1890s) left to be married in the summer of 1906. Miss Julia, a lifelong teacher, remained at Chale from July 1904 until she was transferred to another school in 1913.

An uncertificated teacher, Miss Beatrice Hills, arrived at Chale School in January 1911. She stayed until transferred to another National School on the Isle of Wight, nine years later. Her daily journey from a nearby village was by pony and trap. The pony spent the day in stables at the Clarendon Hotel opposite the school, and the older children attended to its needs there.

Training reforms for teachers now included the award of scholarships and giving of grants for tuition and maintenance. Opportunities were diverse and tailored to meet a wide variety of needs, from elementary to secondary, and including art and technical schools. While a two year course was common, universities also offered a one-year teacher training course following the usual three year degree course. Unqualified teachers, or those who learned 'on the job' (as did Miss Julia) were still to be found, however, until the end of the Second World War. Naturally all the new training, new ideas, new methods brought changes to the subjects taught.

CHAPTER 6

Not just the 3 R's

Curriculum changes with the new Act were vast and beneficial, and indicated not only the changing needs of the workplace, but also showed a change in attitude to education and to the children themselves. Their implementation must have caused as great an upheaval everywhere as did that of the National Curriculum in the early 1990s. Perhaps this was especially true of the scattered rural schools, with few teachers, small premises and very little in the way of equipment. Nevertheless it was done, and Chale's log books give a good account of one small village's efforts.

During the nineteenth century the emphasis had been on the three R's, and these were taught somewhat unimaginatively, concentrating on committing to memory as many facts as possible. The girls were also taught basic practical needlework. The idea from the beginning had been to rear young people who were able to read the Bible, sign their names on the marriage register, and do as much calculation as was necessary for menial work. Sparking imagination, fostering individual talent, or opening doors to enterprise and advancement was not the object. Perhaps the unspoken intention was to reproduce a lower social class better able to carry out the requirements of a higher level of society, but not allow that class to find a place among them.

Though this did not entirely change with the coming of the 1902 Act, gradually the aim became to cultivate reason and imagination in the pupil. The pupil's needs began to be considered, and a more interesting way of encouraging the children evolved.

English became not just grammar, but literature, drama and speech training. History went beyond the dry recitation of dates and battles, to include social, economic, local and imperial changes; the study of famous lives and achievements; and of ancient and Biblical events. As for mathematics, the changes were revolutionary. Syllabuses were widened to cover not only arithmetic, but mechanics, geometry and so on (though usually this was at secondary level).

The methods of teaching progressed, too, bringing in the use of historical maps, literature and illustrations, and visits to monuments and museums. The children's understanding of the subject became important, not just their ability to memorise tables and rules. Problems set were more related to everyday life, and their solving was intended to go some way towards fitting the pupil for his or her on-going career.

Geography, music, art and handicraft received attention and again understanding and imagination were the keynotes. Cookery and personal hygiene became required subjects for girls, gardening and woodwork for boys. The greater funds now available enabled small village schools to widen their scope, though they were often hampered by lack of suitable buildings. Buildings, however, were not required for horticulture, and after a visit to Chale in 1904 a School Inspector reported "The introduction of gardening has had an excellent effect".

The long-standing problem of Christian teaching remained. The Church of England's position was much weakened by the Act, but those in charge continued to fight for their own schools, and for instruction in C. of E. doctrine. This is very evident in Chale's case where scripture lessons were still given daily, the Rector visiting twice a week to take them himself. The whole school (except for those children exempted) continued to go to Church for short services several times a term, and pupils were expected to attend Sunday Services every week. The Diocesan Inspector came annually to examine the whole school on the year's study.

In 1919 the Religious Inspector's report said "The children of this School continue to receive a religious education of high character, which, by God's blessing, must surely have a lasting influence on their lives". Local newspaper reports show also that Chale had long been acquitting itself very well in inter-school scripture competitions. As back as 1891 newspaper reports showed that Chale came second to Newport Girls' School adding "...but when it is noticed that Newport Girls' sent in 22 out of 77 (pupils), while Chale sent in the whole of the scholars, their relative position becomes more equalised".

The new curriculum stressed the need to prepare pupils for the sort of work they were likely to move on to. Local industries had to be studied, and visits made to factories etc in the vicinity. As far as rural education was concerned the emphasis was on the environment, the study of nature, the crops grown, and the effect of geographical features. It was expected that this would create the habit of observation in children, and lead on to an interest in the chemistry of soils, botany etc., especially for boys. At that time lessons were very much gender orientated, and the girls' work concentrated on domestic skills.

Soon after the Appointed Day, Mrs Cooke recorded in the infants' log book "Have introduced Mat weaving, paperfolding, formation of letters on the ballframe as kindergarten subjects..." A month later she adds"...bead threading for the Babies, as an aid in teaching number". While Mr Cooke, dealing with the older children, writes in April 1904, "Observation Lesson in the afternoon on spring flowers, and birds their nests and habits. Route - Downs to Gotten Lane. Standard I and II Geography lesson in sand pit on the cliff". In June the following year, Standards III to VII had an observation lesson when they went to Ladder Chine and did "Land measuring etc".

Cookery was taught apparently long before it became obligatory. The class was mentioned in May 1907, when "Grace M Borthwick HMI visited to inspect the Cooking Class, and found the instruction very useful and practical". The small size of the original schoolrooms, and the primitive conditions make it difficult to see how they managed.

One resident, Mrs Brown, who was at school during the 1st World War, explained the arrangements. About 14 girls would be involved at one time, working in pairs, an older one with a younger. Trestle table tops (which had to be well scrubbed at the end of each lesson) were fitted on to the desks. She said the actual cooking was done in the classroom in a "kitchener", that is a small kitchen range with the fire to one side of the oven (it was also the regular room heater). Firstly they would have a high temperature for pastry-making, while this was cooking, cakes needing less heat were prepared. Meanwhile others peeled vegetables for a stew, to go in with the cakes or just after. Finally, as the temperature dropped to very low, biscuits or shortbread were cooked. Amid gales of laughter, Mrs Brown said "Every Thursday morning we made meals for Mr and Mrs Cooke for the rest of the week". Ingredients were provided by the school (or perhaps Mrs Cooke herself) so naturally the results remained there. The girls had no chance to sample their own products.

The cookery class visited a fruit canning exhibition in 1917. This either shows Chale's advanced ideas, or was just because it took place in the parish, at Pyle. There is no explanation as to why this was held in so under-populated an area, but it may have had something to do with wartime shortages, and the need to preserve food where it was to be found, i.e. in the country.

Mrs Brown also remembered the attention given to needlework, and how she won the annual prize several times. The basics came first "You had to know how to hem, oversew, do seams, buttonholes. For the examination you'd have a piece of material and you would do all these...Then you'd make a garment". Laughing again, she said "Oh...we used to say we sewed for Mrs Cooke and her 2 daughters, Ada and Norah. We made bodices - camisoles we called them. Oh, all the little tucks we used to make!...the needlework was lovely...We made nighties, aprons, tea-towels...dusters I expect to begin with...and handkerchiefs". Fancy embroidery was not part of the syllabus, though Mrs Brown remembered learning "faggoting[xii]which joined two pieces of material together.

Another ex-pupil, Edward Roberts, produced the work his mother (also a former pupil) had done in needlework class. It consisted of samples of patches and darns on a small piece of fabric, in exquisite tiny and regular stitches.

Physical education is not mentioned very often in Chale's records in the early part of the century. "Drill" is occasionally recorded, and there is a surprising entry dated July 1905. The local education committee sent instructions that all children should be taught swimming - sensible enough in a county surrounded by sea. This presented difficulties, not only were there no public pools on the Island, but as Mr Cooke recorded "The shore in this neighbourhood is very dangerous to bathers". Mr Harvey of Chale Farm suggested they use his sheep wash[xiii]. Even more surprisingly, they did! But it was a short-lived arrangement as the natural spring water supply to the sheep wash failed due to drought. By the end of the month the entry read "There appears to be no hope of continuing this season". Swimming was not to re-appear as

---

[xii] Experts will know this as "insertion stitch-twisted".

[xiii] A sheep wash is not to be confused with a sheep dip. The wash wasusually an artificial pool created in a stream, into which the sheep were pushed to clean them before shearing. No chemicals were involved.

part of the curriculum for many years (see page 81). However, the distances the children walked to school no doubt gave them exercise enough, together with their out-of-school activities on the farm, or at sea.

In December 1907 sadness came to Chale school as Mrs Cooke recorded a tragic entry one Monday afternoon. "Death of Scholar. News was received this afternoon of the death of Eva Brown. She was at School on Friday and appeared to be in her usual health, but developed a cold on Saturday and complained that her throat hurt her." Eva had just started school, and was well remembered by her friend, Mrs Downer, aged 91 in 1993.

The school was in the midst of a virulent outbreak of diphtheria which began in September 1907 and spread rapidly. The school was closed by order of the Medical Officer of Health for two weeks in October, reopened, then closed again for 3 weeks at the end of term. The ban remained in force until mid-January 1908, when "14 diptheric (sic) or sore throat cases returned to School", but three more children were infected. Nine more were taken ill the following week, and the infection lingered until Irene Toogood was the last school case in July. One other death was recorded, that of an ex-pupil, Sidney Toogood, aged 18, (probably related to Irene) who died of the infection after a brief illness during the August holidays.

Immunisation now means that this disease is a rarity, but in the early decades of the century it was not uncommon. This particular outbreak could probably have been traced to several sources of infection. Cats and cows can be carriers, and in rural areas such as Chale, children daily came into close contact with these animals. It only needed one child to pick up the infection to pass it on by sneezing, use of the same eating and drinking utensils, or just by proximity. Chale school had over 100 pupils at the time and ventilation in the crowded classrooms was not good, as Mr Blizard's inspection recorded. Desks were usually of the two or four-seater variety (certainly two dual desks were delivered in February 1908), and close contact could not be avoided.

Diphtheria is not carried in water, but former pupils remember that, even 10 years later, there was just one old enamel mug, tied to the tap, from which they all drank. On top of all this it is likely that by their poverty they were not robust children anyway, and as one authority put it "...nothing furnishes such constant and extensive opportunities for personal infection as school attendance"[65].

Eventually the epidemic passed, and that was the last time diphtheria attacked Chale school with such ferocity. A few cases were reported in 1910, one in 1913, but fortunately never again an outbreak on the scale of that in 1907/08.

Other infections, however, streaked through the classrooms, and the first 10 years of the twentieth century saw many outbreaks. The school was closed by the MOH on account of measles in March 1903. Then, following swiftly after the diphtheria, came chicken pox and measles, closing the school for this reason in November and December of 1908. The next spring scarlet fever caused closure. In 1913 it was whooping cough, in 1916 measles and chicken pox at the same time. So it went on, periodically school attendance was decimated by infectious disease, right up to the 1940s. There was, in addition, the odd case of typhoid, scarletina and German measles. No doubt the same factors of over-crowding, poor general health, and questionable hygiene all contributed to the epidemics. Conditions have improved now and with modern preventative methods infectious childish diseases on this scale have been considerably reduced.

Coughs, colds and influenza were very common, and the 'flu epidemic of 1918 struck the school (indeed the village and whole Island) in November. Many of the children suffered a repeat dose in the following spring. This reflected the pattern countrywide, ordinary British people were just not very healthy and had little resistance, especially after the stress and privations of 4 years of war.

In 1906 the Education (Provision of Meals) Act was passed, allowing schools to provide hot midday meals where it was thought necessary, usually in the large cities. Chale children, however, still either brought their own dinner, or walked home to a meal at noon.

An Act to provide medical inspection of children was passed in 1907, though not with the requirement to give treatment where necessary. Medical inspection in Chale was first mentioned on 14 May 1908 (see page 52) when under 5s and over 12s were examined. After that the doctor's visit was recorded about once a year, and heads were regularly checked for lice infestation from 1913. Educational authorities also began to recognise the importance of physical exercise for children and include it in the curriculum.

CHAPTER 7

Attendance, Holidays & Treats

The first monthly attendance return from Chale school was forwarded to the LEA offices on 16 October 1903, and this signalled a change in the early attitude to schooling. The appointment of an attendance officer, another innovation of the 1902 Education Act, brought a new awareness of the need for going to school regularly to both children and parents.

Teachers now found themselves with more administrative work in marking registers, working out attendance averages, explaining absences and sending in weekly and monthly returns. So the log books had such entries as "Owing to wet weather and a little sickness the average for week is decidedly low", and "...attendance is still below the average, but considering the bad weather and the distance 60% of the children come the percentage is very good". The managers were involved, too, as their Correspondent had to certify and sign the registers, once every quarter.

The County Council Education Department enforced the routine, the attendance officer visiting school twice a week to make checks, but rewards were also offered. A note arrived in December of 1903 stating that "...every school which makes 93% attendance during the month may give a half holiday every month." This was quickly put into practice, and for 95% attendance in November the school broke up half a day earlier for the Christmas holidays. In the following year Chale children had a half holiday for April, May, June, July and October's figures, and these holidays were still being recorded occasionally until 1927.

Parents for the most part made much more effort to see their childrenwent to school. Fines (of up to 20 shillings, i.e. probably 2 weeks' wages) and even imprisonment resulted for people who failed to comply. So in very wet weather in February 1904 "...Children attend wonderfully well. Brought in vans" (i.e. horse-drawn covered wagons). But some days travelling was just too difficult and with only a handful of pupils in school the registers were not marked. Even those that did manage the journey were drenched and repeatedly in those early years the log book records "clothes had to be dried".

At Chale, apart from sickness, the reason for absence was often the weather. Before school transport was the norm, former pupils remember that Mrs Cooke kept a box of clothes for wet days. Older girls would help undress, rub down and clothe the little ones in dry garments from this box. The wet things were hung on the fire guard round the range or the "Tortoise" stove so they were ready to put on at the end of the day. This must have contributed to the poor atmosphere in already badly ventilated rooms.

A sad case came to light at this time. One July the attendance officer enquiring into the absence of Winifred Butcher, went in search of her father, said to be working in the fields. Mr Butcher was not to be found, further visits were made in August and November before contact was made and the reason for Winifred's non-attendance discovered. "It is a very difficult case to decide" said the log book "The mother being dead and the father apparently not in a position to support a housekeeper, it necessitates the girl being at home to look after the younger sister, and to keep house while her father is at work". Reading between the lines, it is likely that the man was in the depth of grief, fearful of the legal repercussions of keeping his daughter at home, and at his wits end to know what to do. The ultimate outcome is not mentioned, except to say that the officer "notified the Secretary that it is a case of great hardship". For Winifred this must also have been a traumatic time, both in losing her mother, and in having adult responsibilities suddenly thrust upon her.

The common feeling both among children and parents seems to have been that the attendance officer was a bogeyman. He must indeed have been an imposing figure in his uniform of "patrol jacket with hook and eye; embroidered on Collar in Gilt 'School Attendance Officer'; with 2 pairs of plain trousers, with cap with French peak oakleaf braid band, braided top, silk lining, white head leather and chin straps". This uniform, according to the Education Committee Minute Book, cost £3.13s.3d. per set. The children were coerced to school by the threat of their parents being taken and "locked up" if they did not attend. The reaction of parents in Mr Butcher's situation was often to say nothing, through worry, fear and ignorance, and lay low in the vain hope that the child's absence went unnoticed.

Considerably more went on in Chale school besides lessons. Various "Treats" have been mentioned, and much practice went into the annual concert performed there for the parents. At Christmas a regular party with games followed the prize giving when medals and good attendance certificates were presented. In 1908 Mrs Dabell handed out medals to Lawrence Brooke, Alfred Burt, Charles Wiggins, Harold Brown, Ada Cooke, Nora Cooke and Irene Cheek, and 37 certificates. Prizes were also given for cookery and for needlework. From 1908 the Baring prize is mentioned, this was given each year from 1904, by a very well known and respected member of the Education Committee, Mr (later Sir) Godfrey Baring. Officially it was a Challenge Banner for School Attendance to be awarded to one boy at each of the boys' schools in the county, and Mrs Baring gave a similar prize for girls.

Needlework was judged in May most years. The winner had to be resident in the parish, and a ruling by the managers in 1909 laid down that no girl could win more than three times in her school career. Both these rules must have caused great disappointment. Elsie and Ida Collis won in their respective classes in 1910, but their 5 shillings was withheld because they lived just outside the parish. Happily "The prizes were found by the Master and the second place took the Charities prize. It must have been harder for Irene Cotton the next year "as she had received it three times it was handed to Victoria Brown", and the same thing happened to M Bull and Majorie Linington in other years. Florence Chiverton (nee Downton) was also a winner several times, but eventually a loser. She remembered it with much laughter in the 1990s, "I was the only girl in the group" she said "so it always had to be me".

Prizes were also given following a lecture on "Alcohol" by someone from the Hants. and I.o.W. Union of the Band of Hope, for the childrens' "excellent reproduction of the lesson". This gentleman made an annual visit to talk on such subjects as "Physiological effects of Alcohol", and "Alcohol and the Brain". No doubt he was well-intentioned, but can he really have held the pupils' interest? It does, however, illustrate the continuing concern for moral and religious instruction in the school.

Other regular events were the day closures for excursions. These were, of course, in mid-summer, each religious denomination in the village running its own...the children were no respecters of denominations and made a point of joining their friends for each of these treats. In July 1910 the Bible Christian Chapel held its outing on the 5th, the Wesleyans had a tea-party on the 13th, the Church Band of Hope went on an excursion on the 19th, and the Mission Hall rounded off the season on the 26th. The pattern for these was for the children to be loaded onto "brakes" - horse-drawn vehicles - with a plentiful supply of sandwiches and soft drinks, to travel the few miles to Ventnor, Shanklin or Sandown. There they paddled, bathed and made sand castles, with perhaps games or races after lunch, ending the day by taking a different route home. Simple pleasures, but according to those who remember them, very much enjoyed. After the First World War the treats dwindled, and by 1925 they had ceased, to be replaced by school outings of a similar nature.

The day the mackerel came in in July 1904 provided a wonderful excuse to take all the children staying to dinner, about 70 of them, to the beach. There they helped the local fishermen catch a shoal of the fish, and according to custom each child would have been given 2 mackerel. No doubt this resulted in the reek of fish spreading through the premises by the end of afternoon school, both from the catch and from the children's clothes and hands.

The school was used as a polling station, so every election meant a day off. They had another half-holiday in 1907 for the ceremony of naming the lifeboat. The death of Edward VII closed the school (and postponed the Church Sunday School treat). Royal occasions were always good for a holiday, and though George V's coronation day was wet, still there was a tea in Mr Harvey's barn (Chale Farm), with the presentation of medals and mugs. The funds for this showed an excess of £3.8s.9d., so the children had another tea in the first week of August to use up the money. Point-to-point races and Chale sports both warranted a half-holiday, so did the school's Sale of Work in July 1913. At the latter 16 of the girls "plaited the May Pole, and danced 4 Morris Dances. This was repeated 4 times during the afternoon and evening and was very favourably commented upon by the official County Press reporter who was present".

So passed the early years of the twentieth century. Chale's school was firmly in the centre of village life, few went elsewhere for their recreation. The community enjoyed school concerts, local sports, and similar gatherings. The parish contained all their needs, shops, churches, doctor, friends and relations. Many young people grew up with hardly a thought of leaving the area, and usually with the idea of following in their fathers' footsteps. Once over the upheavals of the 1902 Education Act the school had settled happily under the strict but benign eyes of Mr & Mrs Cooke, the Managers and the Rector, Rev. Heald. The same could be said of other village schools in England, but August 1914 heralded such disturbance, such sorrow, such destruction of the settled order of things that could not have been imagined in the stately, prosperous and unhurried Edwardian days.

CHAPTER 8

Knitting, Gardening & the Great War

Events in Europe in the fateful days of July and August 1914 receive no mention in the school log books. Nevertheless, along with thousands of other villages, Chale saw its young men flock to join up. A picture postcard titled "Some of the Chale recruits" shows 10 young men in best tweed suits, 9 in flat caps, and one sporting a boater[66]. These gangling youths with self-conscious grins, stand in the road between the Church and the Clarendon Hotel, opposite lined on the school wall sit some of the children. The boater and the dresses of the little girls indicate summer, but had they waited to get the harvest in?

At the beginning of the autumn term, in the midst of the early optimism and enthusiasm for the war, the girl pupils at the school collected £2.4s. With that and a donation of £3, material was bought and they set to work to sew for the Belgian Relief Fund. On 9 October "a parcel of 116 garments consisting of frocks, caps, shirts, general underlinen etc all made by the children...was forwarded for distribution to London". They kept up this work through that term and it was reported on 6 January 1915 that 430 garments had been made, and many scarves and "Crimean" (presumably balaclava) helmets knitted for the soldiers. Particularly mentioned were the warm woollen shirts sent to the Chale Scouts on active service[xiv].

No more mention of knitting and sewing for the Forces is recorded, perhaps the novelty of reporting it wore off, but undoubtedly both women and children continued to supply warm garments for the soldiers and sailors. Perhaps also the realities of the war were coming home to residents, and as the telegrams arrived so grief took the bravado out of these activities.

Sons, husbands and sweethearts were lost, but only one family man died. Just before Christmas 1917, Mrs Brown's father was killed. Nearly 80 years on she still remembered the day when she and her older brother were sent home from school to comfort their mother, who had 2 younger children (one only 6 months old). The greatest tragedy, she said, was that he had volunteered though he need not have gone. With immense losses at the time there was great pressure on all able-bodied men to enlist, those who didn't often being labelled cowards.

Another death occurred in September 1918 when the Rector's son died of wounds in France. The event appears in stark, language in the log book. "6 September. The Rector did not take Scripture as he was at Rouen attending his

---

[xiv] Chale had a flourishing scout troop formed soon after the movement started. The founder and first Troop Leader was Captain Scott, who lived at Walpen, and he was followed by John Cooke, the schoolmaster (see page 24)

43

wounded son." And again "13 September. The Rector returned from the funeral on Wednesday. He did not take Scripture during the week".

With these and similar events in the village the lives of relatives and friends at home changed. At that time there was no knowledge of counselling in cases of the trauma of sudden disaster. The community supported one another as well as they knew how.

School continued much as before, although there were fewer Church and Chapel summer outings. Mention was made of the shortage of farm labour, so in June 1917 "Several boys are absent helping to make the hay", and the next year"...some of the bigger boys have been helping to get in the hay. There being so many village men in the Army". In September 1918 on instructions from the Education Committee "Children went blackberrying to get fruit for preserving for the troops". Another item that indicates the scarcity of food records the collection of eggs from Chale, Niton and Whitwell Schools[67]. It is not clear, however, whether this was a regular or one-off event, whether contributions came from the pupils' homes, or whether schools actually kept a few hens.

In Chale's log book little more is recorded in the war years, just the frequent visits of the Rector, and the Attendance Officer. The latter continued to arrive twice a week, doubtless clad in all the imposing splendour of his uniform. How he reached Chale in those days before widespread use of cars is not mentioned. Did he walk? Ride a horse or drive a pony trap? Or did he travel the rough lanes on a bicycle?

Other than these regular events one of the few items noted is that in 1915 two girls (Edith and Marjory Payne) were knocked down by a motor lorry while holidaying in London. The number on roll that year was 87, but in the September Mr Cooke recorded that the total of children of school age in the village was 76. "Formerly" he added "it averaged 120". In March, 1918, many children were complaining of stomach-ache. The headmaster thought that this was "probably owing to war bread".

Gardening took on a new significance in the curriculum. At that time Chale's boys had 12 plots. Frank Reynolds could proudly point out the exact location of his over 70 years later, though the area no longer formed part of the school's grounds.

The Minutes of the County Education Committee add a little more information[68]. They reported some correspondence with Chale on the subject and an interview with the Headmaster in 1914. It was agreed that the Committee would continue to supply seeds, and the Master would take the produce for himself. In return he would charge no rent, and provide manure and gardening tools. The Committee saw the arrangement as advantageous and resolved that it should continue.

Horticultural discussion did not end there. At a conference on the Island in June 1915[69] Schools Inspector Mr Joad said the gardens should be village models but usually were held in derision. Apparently crops suffered repeated and continued failure. Six schools had satisfactory plots, but 9, including Chale's, were not good enough.

Things had not improved by 1916. HMI's report for Chale in that year shows just how much emphasis was set upon growing food[70]. It seems that he was far from satisfied with what he found on his visit. "On plots occupying not more than 1 to 1½ rods"[xv] he said "there should be entire freedom from weeds". He goes into much detail on precise cultivations for the heavy soil, and the variety of vegetables to be grown. To make the garden attractive, the growing of flowers in small quantities was also recommended. The peas that year certainly did not come up to expectations, and the Inspector describes them as "Too thin in the rows and the plants themselves spindly and weak". The written work connected with the subject was not good enough either. The boys were expected to keep pocket books for rough notes to be written up later, together with accounts and scale maps of the plots and their contents. It seems a lot was expected of these 12 - 14 year olds, and Mr Cooke's family can't have dined very well off the produce of his school's gardens.

The report added some praise for Mr Cooke, however, "...theHead Teacher is very keenly interested in the subject". Frank Reynolds differed on this "Mr Cooke didn't know any more than we did" he commented with amusement. Yet interest in the subject led at least one Chale boy, Oscar Sprake, to make a career of horticultural work. Efforts of others in their home gardens in future years made Chale Show one of the most successful on the Island. Incidentally, important as the subject was, girls were not allowed to take part in gardening lessons[71]. Gardening remained on the curriculum at Chale School until the implementation of the 1944 Education Act.

A few further details appear in the minutes of the County Education Committee. The teachers who enlisted are named, with a note that their Army pay was to be made up to full salary in their absence. Mr. Cooke, however, was past military age, and his assistants were women. Some female teachers left to do war work[72] but were not encouraged to do so. Miss Grieves of Wroxall, for instance, requested leave of absence to be a Ward Maid, but was told her present job was more important especially while the school's headmaster was "serving with the colours"[73].

It almost seemed as if life in the school hung in limbo, only the daily necessities being accomplished. The worry, sadness, extra work to fill in for serving men, the shortages of food and educational supplies all joined to make life abnormal, dark and gloomy.

When at last the War was over people throughout the country raised money to put up a variety of memorials both to those who were lost and those who returned, and Chale was no exception. In the school hall hangs a plaque recording 137 names of "Chale men who so nobly, for their country's sake served in the Great War 1914-1919" (see page 86). Of the 24 who did not come back many had been Chale School pupils.

[xv] 1 Rod, pole or perch = (i) a unit of length equal to 5 1/2 yards (ii) a unit of square measure equal to 30 1/4 yards. In metric this equals approx. 5 metres, or 30 sq. metres.

A picture postcard dated 18 July 1920 commemorates the dedication of the inscribed granite cross erected in St Andrews Churchyard[4]. The whole community seems to be there, little girls in white dresses and large hats, young choir boys in surplices, men and women of all ages. From then until the Second World War the school went regularly to Church on Armistice Day, 11 November, for a short service and the two minutes silence. In 1920 a note that would be amusing if it were not so poignant records "The children brought flowers and of the best, three bunches were made. The children at playtime marched to Church and deposited the three bunches at the foot of the Memorial Cross. The remainder of the flowers were deposited by the children on the grave of Albert Rayner...the only person to be buried in the churchyard of the 24 men of the village killed in the War. He was formerly a Chale School scholar". This man was a leading seaman and fell at the Battle of Jutland.

CHAPTER 9

Change of Head Teacher, Medicals & Scholarships

"Retirement of the Head Teacher - 29 September, Mr J Cooke, the Head Teacher retired, having reached the age limit fixed by the Isle of Wight County Education Committee at 60 years. For 31 years he had been Master of this School, being appointed September 28, 1891, and commencing duty on that date. (signed) C W Heald, Correspondent."

Thus ran the log book entry of 1922 that ended Mr Cooke's leadership of Chale school. He had seen many educational changes during his time, particularly the change from Voluntary School to LEA control, and must have felt quite sad that his leading role in the community was now to end.

Mr and Mrs Cooke are remembered with affection for their kindliness and fairness, but from His Majesty's Inspector's point of view it seems they did not always succeed in their teaching methods. With 87 children crowded into two fairly small rooms, this is hardly surprising, and the two reports available damn with faint praise. In 1912 "...the methods and results of Teaching are in general fairly good...reading is fairly good...the geography and history of the first class are not well known...drawing is only fair"[75]. The report for 1914 said "The kindly manner in which the School is conducted gives a good impression...There are however many points to which attention should be drawn and serious endeavours should be made to secure improvement...in the methods adopted"[76]. Both reports continue in this vein and must have been embarrassing for the Cookes, but with the passing of 80 years one can only feel sorry for them, working as they did under very difficult conditions.

The reports of the diocesan inspector of religious studies on the other hand, were very enthusiastic and much more heartening[77]. "Admirable religious work is being done in the School" he said. He also commented on the small number of children being withdrawn from the religious lessons in spite of the option under the "conscience clause". Again in 1916 "It is very pleasing to see how the religious teaching occupies its rightful place, the first in the work of the School". Two years later the Inspector writes "It was a privilege and a pleasure to visit the school again, and to find so much evidence of very valuable religious work being done in it". Obviously Chale continued conscientiously to uphold the original aims of the National Society.

The local newspaper report[78] said Mr Cooke had been a teacher for 47 years (which means he began probably as a pupil-teacher in 1875 at age 13). At a brief ceremony on the day he left, schoolgirl Olive Sprake gave him a clock inscribed "Presented to Mr J Cooke on his retirement, by the scholars at Chale School, September 29 1922". Olive hoped he would like it and that as it struck the hours he would be reminded of happy schooldays in Chale. The Rector spoke highly of the headteacher's work, and the County Council representative, Mr J H Brown, said his religious teaching was "an example for any school of moral and religious training". Mr Cooke was, of course, deeply touched by the gift.

A meeting was held in late September at which local residents decided to open a subscription list in order to give Mr Cooke "some small token of their personal regard and appreciation" (at which there was applause)[79]. A note in the paper a month later announced that there was to be an extension of the period for subscriptions to this fund - but nowhere is a presentation recorded[80]. A General Election occurred about this time, which occupied much space in the next few editions, so perhaps smaller items were squeezed out. There is no doubt, however, of Chale's appreciation of Mr Cooke's years of teaching and the high esteem in which the village held him.

He retired but did not immediately leave the house as Mrs Cooke took over his job, and continued as Head Teacher for a further two years. When it came to her turn to retire, at the end of November 1924, there was another presentation. This was marred by an extremely sad event. The log book entry reads:-

"Mrs Heald the Rector's wife was taken ill in school while making a Presentation to the retiring Head Teacher, and died later in the evening".

So for Chale began the inter-war period, a time not noted for great educational progress, for reasons such as the aftermath of the War, and the poor economic climate, which eventually became the Great Depression of the 1930s. Nevertheless reading the log books, accounts in newspapers, and talking to former pupils, all of whom enjoyed their schooldays, these years appear to have been the heyday of Chale School. Everyone seemed to be trying to put behind them the tragedies of the Great War, and in spite of many deeply mourned losses a spirit of hope prevailed, and the community was trying to rebuild and go forward.

Those who were spared returned to their homes with great relief, but under that there stirred a need to do better for their children. The way forward for this was seen through education, and difficult as it was following the disruptions and upheavals of war, changes began to take place. New ideas were simmering - changes in attitude between children and parents, teachers and children, parents and teachers; the raising of the school leaving age; extension of education to secondary level for all; and once again changes in the curriculum. Teachers became better paid through the introduction of the Burnham scale of salaries in 1920. Development of training and the opportunity for in-service courses improved teaching standards.

An Education Act of 1918[81] finally abolished fees in elementary schools, and raised the leaving age to 14. Children were no longer able to leave earlier by fulfilling certain conditions. Overcrowding resulted in many schools so provision was made for the establishment of senior schools and central schools for older pupils (12 - 14). Entrance to central schools was competitive and intended to "cream off" the brightest pupils and to offer a course of study to suit them for higher grade careers. But these provisions were principally used in urban districts, in rural areas country children continued in the same outdated and crowded buildings for all their school years.

A proposal was put forward for a Central School at Niton for children fom the   neighbouring villages of Chale, Niton and Whitwell. This once again caused agitation, and the Rector wrote to the National Society for advice in August 1920[82]. The problem was that though Chale and Whitwell were Church of England Schools, Niton had a Council School, and Rev. Heald was concerned about "the steps we ought to take to safeguard the Religious Instruction of our children". He was sent a copy of a circular produced by the Society, and advised that "The Local Education Authority has no power to <u>compel</u> (their emphasis) children from Church Schools to attend a Council Central School". In the event the proposal was dropped, and Chale children remained in their own village.

In retrospect this may have been to the children's disadvantageas there were few secondary schools on the Isle of Wight[83]. One school at Sandown was in existence when the County Council took over in 1902, a second was opened in Newport in 1904. No further County secondary schools existed until after the 1944 Act, apart from a Technical College at East Cowes, and Newport Grammar School which offered some free places to children successful in scholarship examinations. With the Island's population standing at just over 82,000 in 1901, rising to approximately 86,000 in 1939, this seems a very poor provision.

Overall the 1902 Act began the decline of Church influence on small rural schools. The Church authorities tried to retain power, but the financial advantages of coming under the new Local Education Authorities prevailed.

As early as 1838 Diocesan Boards of Education had been set up, one of their aims was to establish training schools for teachers, and another was to assist in the establishment, maintenance and inspection of elementary schools. These boards continued until 1870. They were followed by the Diocesan Committee of Education set up in 1889, which became the new Diocesan Board of Education (1893 - 1915). This was intended to encourage both religious and secular education in schools and to provide funds. Next (between 1921 and 1928) a Church Council of Education was formed. So over the '20s and into the '30s the voice of the Established Church became weaker and weaker, its various committees, councils and boards were short-lived and had little say in elementary education[84].

Meanwhile the state became more involved in all types of provided and voluntary schools. A consultative committee reported on "Education of the Adolescent" (the Hadow Report) in 1926[85]. Their findings included suggestions for the division of education into three levels, (infants (5 - 7), juniors (7 - 11), and seniors (11 - 14/15), and the raising of school leaving age to 15. It was not until many years later that these became law. So yet another generation of children, including those at Chale, spent all their school life at one inadequately equipped school.

The Education (Administrative Provisions) Act of 1907 made it obligatory (amongst other things) for LEAs to provide medical inspection of all children attending public elementary schools (as already mentioned). During the first forty years of the twentieth century much was done to improve children's health, responsibility for this being delegated to the Minister of Education by the Minister of Health. The actual work was carried out by medical and nursing staff employed by the local education authorities. Dr J A Gibson was the first Medical Officer appointed on the Isle of Wight (in 1908)[86]. His salary was to be £400 p.a., including travelling expenses. Managers from Chale School wrote to say they felt this was too much, but their objections were overruled.

Sometimes local benefactors paid for provision of spectacles, and the Minutes of the I W Elementary Education Committee record several such instances. In other cases arrangements were made for education at special schools for those with physical or mental disabilities. So in those early years Island children were sent to schools at Hampshire, Kent and even Devon[87]. For children to be sent far from home and parents, in a time when communication was not easy, must have brought them much emotional distress even if the motives behind the placement were intended for the child's benefit. At least two children from Chale did indeed spend part of their school life at Lord Mayor Treloar School, at Alton, Hants., where they received orthopaedic treatment.

Following the first medical inspections recorded at Chale (see page 38), the log book refers to the doctor's "Annual visit". The school's cramped conditions made medical inspection day one of considerable disruption. It is recorded that examinations took place in one or other of the classrooms, in the sitting room of the Master's house, in the W.I. Hall, and even on one occasion in a room at the Clarendon Hotel opposite. A note in the CC Minutes records that "...the necessary stripping would create a certain amount of opposition among parents, especially in country districts". It was much regretted that some parents viewed the inspection with distrust and suspicion[88].

The local district nurse called several times a week, and her chief preoccupation was with head lice. One unfortunate family at Chale was frequently sent home because of "dirty heads", probably not their fault but due to the poor living conditions still prevailing among some farm workers. Nevertheless, what humiliation! Infestation still occurs occasionally in the 1990s, but modern hair washing preparations, combined with improved living standards, usually quickly control an outbreak. The nurse was also on hand to deal with playground accidents, cut knees or fingers, or to carry out routine treatments, like syringing ears and repeat dressings.

Dental inspection was first mentioned in the summer of 1926, and on a regular basis after that. A good many cavities seem to have been found, on one visit in 1928 the dentist treated 10 girls and 15 boys. A few years later "School Dentist spent the day in school giving dental treatment (39 children attended)", and he came again on the following 2 days to complete the work. On 31 August 1938 "Bernard

Young's attendance withdrawn this morning. He went home after reaching the dentist's room". Presumably this means that at least one child did not appreciate such provision.

Poor dental health was again an indication of conditions existing at the time. General knowledge of diet was considerably less than it is today, and nearly everyone used too much sugar. Considerations of expense (for toothbrushes and paste) as well as ignorance sometimes meant children did not clean their teeth[89]. Private dental treatment had to be paid for, too, quite apart from the transport difficulties in reaching a dentist from rural areas. It was, therefore, only in cases of extreme pain that professional attention was sought.

Every child going on a school "journey" had to have a medical inspection before departure. Bright children who gained a scholarship to the secondary school were also medically examined before admittance. At Chale a number of children appear to have been treated for various ailments or defects, no precise details are, of course, given, but such pupils are often referred to as "specials", and the doctor's visit to them was frequently recorded.

Children must have thought that apart from lessons, life consisted of inspections and examinations. The examinations went beyond the physical, too. Exams. in school work every term (or "terminal" tests as the log writer quaintly called them), the three part scholarship examination (parts 1 and 2 in school, part 3 in Newport), and annual diocesan examinations in religious knowledge were all part of the school year. Competition was keen for acceptance at secondary school, and it was greatly to the credit of Chale's teachers (considering the difficulties they worked under) that in most inter-war years two or three scholars gained a place. A few of these children did not take up the opportunity as parents were unable to afford to keep them in school for the extra years of secondary schooling.

CHAPTER 10

Stepping into a wider world

As for the curriculum, domestic skills were still considered important for the girls, perhaps because in the aftermath of war the country was trying to struggle back to former "normality". October 10, 1919, records "Nurse Blackler gave a demonstration to senior girls of the latest method of washing and dressing a very young baby. Mrs Cooke's life sized doll was used in the lesson." This post-war log entry was followed, in January 1921, by a note regarding cookery classes, which took place while boys were taught gardening. Some confusion over the lessons had arisen in the light of the proposed Central School at Niton, and when no Cookery register appeared that term, the staff "considered that the subject would be taught at Niton". However, this was sorted out by the Director of Education who called to say the notice concerning cookery did not apply to Chale. Classes were reinstated right away.

New subjects and new attitudes were appearing at this rural school, as doubtless throughout the country. The inspector's report for July 1921 mentions "A modification of the Montessori Method[xvi] of teaching has been partially introduced". He adds that more apparatus than that made and supplied by the teacher would be necessary before the method could be fully adopted.

Educational day trips became more numerous in the decade 1920-30, the older children visiting such places as Carisbrooke Castle on the Isle of Wight, Portsmouth and Winchester. Participation in local shows and festivals, e.g. Country Dance Competitions, Chale Show, the Island Annual Horticultural Show, was encouraged. A collection of vegetables from the school gardens was entered for the latter and the Challenge Cup was won more than once (obviously horticultural standards had risen). Regularly at the school prize-giving ceremony certificates, medals and books were still being handed out for attendance, good work etc. Needlework prizes for the girls continued to be supplied in cash from the Chale Charities. Nature walks became more numerous, giving country children greater awareness of their environment as was recommended in preparation for their expected occupations in life.

Whatever happened at national level, in Chale School religion remained an important part of the curriculum, and scripture lessons were given by the rector twice a week. Children were still required to attend church every week, and on special

---

[xvi] This referred to Dr Maria Montessori, 1869-1952), who allowed her pupils to move about instead of sitting in rows. She found that even tiny children, while being kept within the bounds of acceptable social behaviour, were happily occupied working with simple apparatus on their own. Discipline was natural and free as in a well-ordered community of adults.

festivals with the whole school except those specifically withdrawn under the Conscience Clause. Every year the children sat a Scripture examination, the prize being a Bible presented by the Religious Tract Society[90]. Several reports on this examination survive for the 1930s and make interesting reading. In November 1935 the Rector of a neighbouring village was examiner, and he said: "...There was evidence here of painstaking teaching conscientiously given. The children were responsive and not by any means ignorant. The result of the examination was that Ruby Harding came out easily first; but as she had been given the Bible last year, the names of the second and third are mentioned, viz. Norah Parker and Chrissie Coward."

The syllabus for that year was:-
1. Jesus, the Son of God, and Saviour of men.
2. The Bible and what it is, especially the Old Testament.

Another year children were examined on "The Gospel according to St Luke", and in 1938 "The Bible and what it is, with special reference to the New Testament books and their writers" and also "St John's Gospel, its aim and special characteristics, with certain passages memorised". Examples like this show just how seriously the subject was taken, and the depth at which it was studied, even among the very young.

Further correspondence with the National Society records an exchange dated July 1922[91]. The rector was most concerned about the appointment of a new teacher and asks if the managers had the right to demand the appointment of a member of the Church of England. The LEA apparently were advertising for an "assistant non-certificated teacher", no mention of church membership. The applicant in question was a "keen energetic Wesleyan" and his appointment would mean the younger children were under "...Non-conformist influence. What steps do you advise in the matter?" A supplementary teacher already in post was said to be a Pentecostal Christian, and the Reverend Heald was very worried - perhaps his agitation accounted for his forgetting to sign the letter. He was told that the 1902 Act did not "compel managers to have no regard to the denomination to which the teacher belongs when appointing an assistant teacher", and it was suggested that the managers place their own advertisement, specifying C of E membership.

The summer outings and treats run by the various religious bodies in Chale (see page 41) became fewer in the 1920s. The Wesleyan Sunday School excursion still merited a day's holiday, but the Bible Christians, the Blackgang Mission and St Andrews Church of England are not mentioned. These are remembered in the 1930s so probably took place during half-term, or other school holidays, or on Saturdays. In any case attendance at both the Mission and the Bible Christians was in decline[92].

Many people who were at school at the time still recall Churchoutings with much pleasure, the trip to Sandown or Ventnor being a great novelty to them. Sylvia Greville (nee Whittington) remembers tea at the Sunday School room in Sandown. She said there were "masses of people at trestle tables, and after tea everyone went to the canoe lake. That was the big thing, to go on the boating lake and have a bottle of pop."

The change may also have had something to do with the Rector. The Rev. C W Heald was replaced in 1927 and a new incumbent (like a new teacher) probably meant new ideas. Perhaps also, the Rev. Heald had lost heart in these jollifications following the loss of his son and his wife.

By contrast, royal occasions still meant days off. Besides Coronation Day each June, a holiday was given for Princess Mary's marriage in 1922, and the Duke of York's in 1923. Empire Day in May was if not actually a day off, still one for celebration and certainly different. A serious but cheerful jingoism prevailed - at least in Chale - where the day was regularly observed "by singing patriotic songs on the lawn and decorating school with flags and daisies". Parents also attended this occasion. It seems laughable now that the Empire has gone and allegiance is supposedly turned to Europe, but patriotism and being British was very important at the time.

Some of the old problems still existed. Measles, mumps, whooping cough and chicken pox made their periodic appearance, and closed the school on several occasions. At that time brothers and sisters of the sufferer were also excluded for a quarantine period of about 3 weeks, so numbers in class reduced rapidly when an outbreak occurred. Influenza and colds were rife, scabies and ringworm as well as lice were noted now and then. Living and school conditions had not improved much and infection spread rapidly.

Normal attendance was better, with the Officer still calling regularly once or twice a week. Even as late as 1925, however, one Chale child was reported for "staying away from school to work for Cotton - baker - on Friday afternoon", and another was mentioned as being a very poor attender.

This decade brought a move towards more involvement of the parents in their children's education. In 1927 the first parent governor (or manager) in the country was appointed (but not in Chale). Lack of Managers' Minute Books for this period, makes it impossible to say when the first parents joined Chale's managers. It is likely that it was many years later, but now education had filtered through so that the parents were more knowledgeable and articulate than those of the 19th century, and liaison between families, teachers and managers was improving. Mr Mew, the Managers' correspondent, called frequently to check the registers, see that all was well with the staff and talk to the children.

The number of children on roll in the 1920s varied between 66 and 83, reflecting the labour intensive agriculture, and the continuation of the full-time coastguard service locally. No mention of improvements in the school buildings appears. Various chairs, tables and dual desks arrived, and in 1928 "A framed picture for use in school" was received, three new desks are recorded, and the fences were mended, but otherwise little work on the fabric is mentioned. Conditions must have progressively deteriorated.

Classes were crowded, and staff were few. In 1925 Miss Pike, headteacher, taught the upper standards, Miss Rowson had Standards I to III, and Miss Beardsall took the Infants[93]. Teachers in most village schools expected to deal with various age groups within the same class, as indeed continues today. In the '20s each teacher at Chale had between 25 and 30 children involving a multitude of different abilities and needs.

Great difficulties arose if anyone was unwell. At one time both Miss Rowson and Miss Beardsall fell ill. One supply teacher was sent but she left on Miss Rowson's return, and Miss Pike writes in the log "For eight weeks I have had to teach Standard II - VII while the junior teacher has had to take the Infants and Standard I, a class to which she is not used. Although a 'supply' could have been obtained the Director would not allow one to come." Miss Beardsall returned after 11 weeks absence, but then Miss Rowson went sick, then both were away again, and for one day Miss Pike reports "I had all children in big schoolroom".

The two years of Miss Pike's leadership do not seem to have been wholly successful, perhaps because of the staff problems. An Inspector's report mentions a visit in 1927 when the older children's work showed "little merit" and "they seemed to take not the slightest interest".

At this time, too, several old boys remember something very alarming, possibly connected with teacher absences and consequent lack of supervision. It concerned the boys' urinal (see page 31) which drained under the playground to the brick culvert still visible opposite the Clarendon Hotel. Apparently a "rite of passage" for the boys was to crawl through this drain to the exit on the road. One man who had done it said it narrowed quite markedly in the middle. He being a skinny little thing wriggled past easily. Boyish bravado no doubt sent many through, but what if a child had an attack of claustrophobia in there? Or got stuck? Never mind the state of their clothes after the trip. Pupils of later years make no mention of this, so presumably it was a short-lived escapade.

Miss Pike was followed briefly by Miss Whitehouse, and then by Miss V C Martin (1928-1935). These new teachers may also have had some influence on changes. They were college trained and much younger than the Cookes, no doubt with more energy and ideas in keeping with their generation. Miss Martin certainly brought fresh enthusiasm to the task. She ran the school together with her sister, Miss K Martin, and they caused a stir among the more traditional villagers as they used a powerful motorbike to expand their social life and improve on the rural bus service.

In less than a year (the Inspector reported) Miss Whitehouse "has affected a radical change and brought new life into the School" (February 1928). Her successor, Miss Martin, and both her assistants were said to be "anxious to do their best for the children and it is satisfactory to note that...steady progress has generally been made."

Towards the end of Miss Martin's time the school milk scheme was introduced. Milk was supplied "by Mr Sprake of Chale at a special rate" (probably

½d per third of a pint i.e. less than half of today's 1p. for 0.2 litre). Within a month 36 children were having milk at mid-morning break.

As the new decade approached, with the slump in agriculture, trade depression, and much unemployment, life in Chale, as in small villages everywhere, was poverty-stricken. The sense of community still flourished, but there was a widening gap between church and school, and the headteacher was sometimes pulled two ways.

Miss Esther A Loosemore was appointed in April, 1936, and remained until the end of 1947, by which time she had married and had two children. The shortage of teachers after the War probably accounted for her being allowed to continue after marriage, and even after the arrival of her family.

Miss Loosemore's reign seems to have been a happy one. Talking of her memories in later years, she frequently went into gales of laughter. She said she was very young, under 30, when appointed, and seemed to think it was a knowledge of bookbinding that got her the job. Her memories of divided loyalties between herself and her school, the Rector, and the County Education Office (the Office) are a fair intimation of problems arising between Church and State over education.

The rector would turn up, she said, and demand that the children were in Church on such and such a day for this or that festival. She would not agree until she had cleared it with the Office. Miss Loosemore also found herself occasionally at odds with local people. With the great competition existing for places at the Island secondary schools, at one time she had to defend herself as some in the community decided that her poor teaching was the reason Chale children seldom qualified. She addressed a managers' meeting on the subject, and was able to show them how few children could reach the required standard whatever school they attended.

Nevertheless her entries in the log book include all sorts of journeys, outings, and nature walks, that show just how concerned she was for the extension of the children's knowledge beyond the confinement of the school building and their home village. Every Christmas the school party, the concert and the prize-giving were reported as happy and successful occasions. She said (with much amusement), however, that the concerts were truly awful as she didn't feel she had a talent for that sort of thing. Children and parents enjoyed them nevertheless, and they helped to bring everyone together in celebration of Christmas.

Lack of money held back educational reforms by central government, though several minor improvements were put forward. Nevertheless good times are still remembered. Occasions concerning Royalty meant everyone met either in sorrow or in celebration and events frequently centred on the school. Much more information about Chale School is available for the years 1930-1940. Many local people supply first hand memories, the Inspectors' reports have been preserved, though still the lack of Managers' minute books leaves a big gap concerning the administrative side.

At national level many changes and new ideas were being discussed. Not least among these was an Education Act of 1936 which raised school leaving age to 15, the date for this change was set for first of September, 1939. The demand for secondary education for all was increasingly discussed. Meanwhile Britain moved inexorably towards the Second World War and in the disastrous summer of 1939 the 1936 Act was suspended.

"Goodalls", Pyle Shute, Chale. Master's residence and site of Chale Charity School. (Area to right of right hand chimney is a 1930's extension).

Chale C.E. Primary School, 1992

Chale School Group, 1900's

Chale School Girls, 1920's. (Hats were made in needlework class).

Mr and Mrs J. Cooke – Retirement Photograph, 1922

Chale School Group 1936

Chale School Group, 1930's

Chale Charities Board – now hanging in school entrance hall.

Chale School Group 1950's

Chale School Group 1950's

Chale School Group with Staff, mid-1960's.
Headmaster, Mr W. Eccleston, centre back row.

Chale School, early 1970's. Mr W Eccleston (left); Mrs Eccleston (far right)
Miss Gallop, next to Mrs Eccleston on right.

Chale School and Staff, 1976

PC Dave Gurd entertains and instructs 1976

Some of Miss Gallop's class prepare to clear the path to the bus shelter,
Environment Week, May 1991.

The road exit of the culvert under the playground, today (see page 55).

All the pupils of Chale School with Mrs Sporne (left),
(centre) Mrs Munn (ancillary), Miss Gallop (right). January 1993.
Reprinted courtesy of Isle of Wight County Press

Trip to Havenstreet Railway, September 1993.

Events in School playground, 25 September 1993

St. Andrew's Church, Celebration Day, 25 September 1993.

Retirement of Miss Gallop, 1998.
Photograph reproduced courtesy of IW County Press.

CHAPTER 11

Gasmasks & more Gardening

The approach of World War 2 was signalled in Chale, as in schools nationwide, nearly a year before war was declared. The log book entry for 2nd December 1938, reads "At eleven o'clock this morning a talk about gas masks and care thereof was given to the school". Gas mask and air raid drill and talks on Safety First then became part of the curriculum. Few children's gas masks were treated with the care parents and teachers expected as they came in handy as markers for rounders bases or goal posts. The regular fitting and adjustment of them also caused a diversion in class as children set out to compete in producing the loudest "raspberry" by blowing hard instead of breathing normally. Miss Loosemore took the senior pupils on the last School Journey for some years in the summer term of 1939. The party of Head Teacher and 7 children left on 3 July for 4 days in London.

In the autumn, war or no war, schooling had to continue as routinely as possible. Things hardly changed in the first few months. Black-out curtains had to be put up everywhere, in Chale this made the dark lanes even darker. Down the centre of the road a white line was painted - some local residents said it was then easier to follow the road home at night! Adults took up war work at First Aid Posts, as Air Raid Wardens or in the National Fire Service, so were extra busy making village social events difficult. The blackout, too, meant that Guy Fawkes night was out of the question. As spring arrived and the situation became more menacing, the likelihood of disruption by enemy action made forward planning almost impossible.

Early in May, 1940, workmen started on a school air-raid shelter, completing it by 24th May. It was constructed under the playground, just on the south side of the vehicle entrance, and a few days after it was finished hurricane lanterns for lighting were received. Then, of course, air raid drill began in earnest and the children (around 70 of them) soon learnt to down books and be inside the shelter within 2½ minutes.

As June arrived things were hotting up across the Channel. Portsmouth and Southampton (important as ports and Naval bases), the radar station at Ventnor, and factories and shipbuilding yards elsewhere on the Island all drew the attention of enemy bombers. Innocent and isolated as Chale was, it still caught the back-lash of the action. So air raid drills were frequent, and on the 18th of that month the log book records "Stirrup pump drill was taken this evening". The time of day suggests that this was for staff only, but no doubt the older boys and girls also knew how to use such a pump.[xvii]

On 20 June the children had a history lesson in the shelter, then on 3 July the real thing. "The school was taken to the air raid shelter during air raid warnings this morning". After that the log book records 51 trips to the shelter until November 1940 when the entry reads "Air raid shelter flowing with water. Children remained in classroom during the warnings." This perhaps indicates some degree of panic or haste on the Local Authority's part when the shelter was installed, as local people knew very well that numerous springs flow through that area from St Catherine's Down. Eight more raids are mentioned over the rest of the term, none after that. The County Clerk called to examine the shelter in February 1941, and that was the end of the matter. After the war it was dismantled, and the playground re-instated.

No doubt there were numerous other occasions when one of the air raid wardens bicycled through the village blowing a warning whistle either at weekends, during holidays or at night[xviii]. Ear plugs were distributed to the children in November, possibly as daylight attacks were replaced by night raids that frequently disturbed sleep. Children from outlying districts were sometimes kept at home during the perilous days of the Battle of Britain as the journey to and from school became too dangerous.

Other incidents add to the records of war at that time. An assistant master, Mr R B Colton, was called for Military Service in 1940 and was replaced by a "Temporary Uncertificated Assistant Mistress". There followed, as in many other schools, months of lesson disruption, as staff left to take up war work or to join the forces. The Headmistress, Miss Loosemore, valiantly coped with a succession of temporary teachers, often managing completely alone aided only by volunteers, including the rector, parents, Miss Loosemore's housekeeper (a former pupil) and various others.

Nevertheless, the usual school activities of prize-giving, concerts and Christmas dinners and parties were kept up. A flourishing youth club was started, and met in the school. An invitation to join the young people was extended by Miss Loosemore to Commandos training locally, as they had nowhere to go in the evenings, and this appears to have been a great success. The school activities were still supported as enthusiastically as possible, though some had to take place in the afternoon rather than after dark.

Very little is recorded about the curriculum at that time. History repeated itself as gardening again became an important subject, Miss Loosemore mentions it frequently. "Digging for Victory" was essential and besides the school gardens which

---

[xvii] Just a small affair, about the size of an old fashioned motor tyre inflater, with a bucket of water and a small hose it was widely used to extinguish incendiary bombs.
[xviii] The all clear was signalled by the warden cycling round ringing a large hand bell.

ran behind Church Place[xix] the children cultivated ground across the road (part of Church land). Under the guidance of Mr T Sprake, pupils did much better than in the First World War producing vegetables in abundance. Further lessons were given by the County Horticultural Instructor who visited the school. One afternoon he "gave a demonstration in grafting". In addition, Miss Loosemore took everyone out blackberrying each autumn term, and made quantities of jam.

Of course, the three "R"s were still important, and the senior pupils were taken to Ventnor Senior School to be taught woodwork (boys) and cookery (girls). Even in May 1940 the headteacher took some of the children for Nature walks on the Downs. After that no mention of walks occurs that summer - later in the month history and geography lessons during a whole week concentrated on "France".

The following year when daylight raids had more or less ceased the head teacher resumed class outings to the Downs. The children went blackberry picking with her in September 1943, as the school building reached 100 years old - but there is no hint that this anniversary was noted.

Normality was also retained as the attendance officer continued to call, and either the correspondent (Mr Mew) or the rector inspected and signed the register. This, incidentally, had to be done on a day chosen at random with no previous arrangement made with the school.

Food was very short in the 1940s, and the Headmistress became aware that the bigger boys, growing fast and ever hungry, had eaten all their sandwich lunch at mid-morning break, and were demanding a share of smaller boys' sandwiches at lunchtime. She, therefore, decided to offer cooked school dinners, the first being provided on 4 September 1941. Much of the produce from the school allotments went into these, as also did jam from September blackberry expeditions, and any other surplus fruit grown locally and given to the school. Plums and apples figured largely for pudding and in this agricultural district rabbits, boiling hens, and perhaps a few eggs sometimes found their way to the school kitchen, besides the rations allowed by the Ministry of Food. Shortage of crockery and cutlery was a problem, so the children brought their own, and washed them up at the conclusion of the meal. Dinner had to be eaten in the classroom using desks for tables, the sloping lids levelled by the insertion of a book. Many official visitors sampled the novelty of these hot dinners provided in a rural school .

Other details in log book entries give clues to wartime conditions. Mrs New (mother of a pupil) took First Aid classes, an army officer talked about dangerous military objects (probably after the departure of the Marine Commando Unit stationed in Chale), and holidays were granted "for effort made in National Savings". VE Day celebration meant a day off, VJ Day occurred in summer holidays, and the whole community joining in festivities. Some years older boys helped with the autumn potato harvest, but there was not the shortage of farm workers as in the 1st World

---

[xix] The land behind Church Place was sold to Mr F Reynolds in the 1960s. He lived at Renwood, Church Place, and wanted to extend his garden at the time.

War. As the War Memorial shows, the loss of life among village men was also not nearly so great and so devastating. Only 6 names were added and these men were, of course, greatly mourned including the two Home Guards who died following an accident during an exercise.

Even after fighting stopped echoes of the War were being recorded. November 5th, 1945, meant a welcome return of Guy Fawkes celebrations. Tea and a bonfire were shared with some Dutch children staying at Billingham Manor. Meanwhile rations remained short and the following year Canada sent a gift of cocoa for the children, and various food parcels came from New Zealand. Pig swill and salvage were still collected. Even as late as 1948 a child (Philip Ablitt) suffered a bite from a rat when he was picking up the pig swill bucket, and the Pest Control Officer had to be called in. In 1949 the salvaged waste paper brought a payment of 3 shillings (15p).

In spite of the war, changes to the education system were going ahead. Another milestone Act was hammered out by Mr R A Butler and passed in 1944. It provided secondary education for all at long last, endorsed raising school leaving age to 15 and envisaged the further raising of it to 16. Many more interested parties and pressure groups had had a say in this bill. The 1902 Act had been the work of an upper social class making provision for the basic education of the working classes. In the 1940s such bodies as the Trades Union Congress, National Union of Teachers, and members of the Labour Party (through their own Members of Parliament) took part in discussions and lobbied for their own people. So the issue was one of great public debate at all levels of society. By then many influential people had themselves experienced elementary education at first hand, and subsequently climbed the ladder to take office at both local and national level. Their opinions and experience were, therefore, very relevant.

The Hadow Report on the education of the adolescent (1926) had resulted in the idea of division into primary, secondary and tertiary levels by age. A huge problem in implementing the 1944 Act was the scarcity of trained teachers, many still in the forces, some having had their training disrupted, others never having had the opportunity to begin as they went straight from school to war work. Lack of buildings also hampered progress as a great number of schools had been destroyed by bombs. In addition the raising of school leaving age would mean many more young people to be catered for. A crash one year training course for teachers was arranged, and building schools (together with homes) became a priority.

As the required changes were made, small rural schools still carried on much as before, except that their older pupils moved on to another school, often some distance from home. The earliest mention in Chale's records came on 5 February 1945 when "15 Seniors were transferred to Ventnor Senior Council School" (6 miles distant), which meant the numbers on roll fell considerably.

At this point Chale school had yet another change of name to become (as today) a C. of E. Controlled Primary School.(see page4). The name of Senior Schools also changed to Secondary Modern Schools. What had previously been called the Scholarship exam, now became the "ll plus" (referring to the age at which all children sat it). Those that passed went to Grammar or High schools and followed a more academic course of study, leading to 'O' and 'A' levels. The others went to Secondary Modern Schools.

Two more results of this Act contributed to change in the village community. Parental loyalties became divided as they possibly had children at two different schools, with school events at each place to be supported - one of which may have been difficult to reach as car ownership immediately post-war was not the norm. The other change came as the Church's influence on the community's children continued to weaken. One Rector was even heard to say that with the 1944 Act "The Church sold its soul". The idea had been that naturally, and of course, all teachers would show allegiance to a Christian Church, in the event a more secular shift occurred. A daily act of worship was compulsory at all schools, but no particular doctrine was to be taught, and in addition there was no requirement for teachers to be practising members of a Church. Indeed many of the new teachers were agnostic or convinced non-believers, perhaps as a result of their recent wartime experiences. At the primary level, C of E schools continued much as before, though the teaching of creed and catechism and regular church attendance was no longer demanded. In Chale the rector called 2 or 3 times a week as usual, regularly took scripture lessons and the children went to Church once or twice a term, but his hold on the children and the community as a whole was less strong. General attendance at Church began to fall off throughout the country, though at this time the parish of Chale still had an incumbent to itself, not sharing with other villages.

CHAPTER 12

Picking up the Pieces in a new Era

For many years the school had regularly sat the Diocesan Scripture exam, reports of which are available from 1919. The last one recorded in the log book took place on 2 May 1947. The Director of Religious Education (Canon T Grigg-Smith) reported on that occasion:

> "This is a particularly happy little school. Both groups of pupils are making effective progress and the subjects of instruction have been suitably treated in themselves and also welded into the greater pattern of life within the Church. The work would be greatly helped by the provision of a large sandtray for the younger children and of a number of wall pictures to illustrate the lessons. It is a great pleasure to visit the school and to converse with such responsive and well-informed pupils. Their teachers have completely won their confidence"

One more report is preserved, for 12 May 1952, but this seems to concern an inspection rather than an examination. Until 1941 Bibles from the Religious Tract Society were given regularly as prizes. In later years examinations recorded refer just to the ll+, at which the rector often acted as invigilator.

Meanwhile throughout the country relationships between children, parents and teachers were again changing. In the early days of universal education, both parents and pupils were under the thumb of teachers, managers, parish priests and possibly other local dignitaries. Later, parents and school authorities acted together to do what was considered best for the children. The first evidence of this in Chale occurred in February 1948, when the log book records "This afternoon about 30 parents came to school to see their children 'at work'. Mrs Brown, Mr Sinclair (Rector), Mr Mew were also present". A month later "...a Parent-Teacher Meeting was held at the school". From then on such evenings (often with a speaker on an educational subject) and visits during lesson time were frequent. A more democratic atmosphere existed, and perhaps the teacher, priest and managers ceased to be such god-like figures.

Wartime conditions meant that few repairs, little redecoration, and certainly no major extensions were carried out over the 6 years, 1939-1945. Men and materials were limited and all efforts went into reconstruction. Little old rural schools were very low on the list of priorities, so the fabric and surrounds of Chale school deteriorated.

Mrs Twyman (nee Loosemore) said the playgroundwas dreadful "all rubble, stones and gravel". A lot of money had been spent just before the war to build a shelter between the boys' and the girls' playgrounds. "Lovely to look at" said Mrs Twyman "all wired glass, but put together boys, stones and nothing to do and what do you get?". Another former teacher, Miss Sibley, also remembered that playground, "...Facing the prevailing wind, and covered with loose gravel, you can imagine what it did to the knees. I smelt permanently of Dettol". She also said they had to go out there to do PE at 10 o'clock each morning "nearly always, it seemed, in the teeth of a strong South Westerly blowing up the Channel". The school had no playing field then as today, that came with major alterations in the 1960s.

The winds are a permanent feature of Chale weather. During one gale, as Miss Sibley was teaching, the rotted wood round the classroom window finally gave way and the window blew in. Splinters of glass scattered all over the room and she had to brush it out of the children's hair, fortunately none of them was hurt.

The run-down conditions included an antiquated heating system. Miss Sibley's first task on arriving in school in winter was to light the fires, four of them. The kitchen-cum-staffroom fire was first, then the Tortoise stove in the south classroom, next the one in the other larger classroom, and finally stoke up another "immense Tortoise stove with a huge great water tank beside it". Even with all this effort the school was often reported to be too cold for the children to work. And there was the exciting day during the terrible winter of 1947 when the children were sent home at dinner time because the Tortoise stove "showed signs of catching the school on fire".

One other early morning task for Miss Sibley was to "de-slug" the wash basins. Great black slugs used to come up the waste pipes overnight and these she said gave the children "the screaming heebie-jeebies". To get all this done and prepare for morning lessons Miss Sibley used to arrive by bus each morning at 8.15a.m.

As for the toilets, set apart from the main building on the eastern boundary, they were actually in the same place as to-day but there the similarity ends. Conditions described in the 1902 report were much the same after the war, though the earth closets had been replaced by chemical toilets, and a few more taps were installed around the school. A schools' inspector's report of March 1952, mentions that these facilities had been recently modernised when the school went on to a septic tank system. However, it was still necessary to go outside to reach the toilet block.

Mrs Twyman left the school at the end of December 1947, and a temporary head teacher was in charge for the spring term. Mrs Wood (a widow) then took up her duties after Easter, and lead the school for the next 12 years. She is remembered as a more worldly-wise, much smarter, even flamboyant person than any teacher Chale had encountered before. Miss Sibley said when she appeared for interview she wore her hair in a bun, had no make-up, and was quietly dressed. As she was well-qualified she got the job. It was only later that the very generous and showy side of her nature was seen. "She sort of hit Chale like a bombshell... she was more sophisticated ... full of beans and a very good teacher" according to Miss Sibley. Mrs Wood's methods were very successful, and parents soon brought children from Niton and surrounding areas as Chale became popular. The school always had an excellent supply of up-to-date books, and the reason for this became clear when in June 1954 Mrs Wood married Mr Green, the County Librarian.

Much is recorded in log books showing the wide range of activities in the school post-war. Once rationing eased Mrs Green regularly organised the baking of school Christmas cakes. Every child brought part of the ingredients and one morning in November was given over to the mixing, everyone joining in.

The Dabells of Blackgang continued to support the school, and the name is often mentioned among lists of guests at prize giving. The Chine was (and still is) a popular venue for summer outings. Various distinguished visitors arrived to give lectures (among them in July 1957 was the poet Mr Alfred Noyes) and film shows on such varied topics as "Wild life in New Zealand", "Children in Jamaica" and "School Life in France". National and Royal occasions were celebrated. A special victory service was held in June 1946 (in Mrs Twyman's era) when the rector distributed messages from the King to all the children. In coronation year, the headteacher arranged for the whole school to visit the cinema to see the film "Elizabeth is Queen", and a week later a party of 22 children and 26 adults went to London to tour the Coronation route, followed by a 3-hour trip on a river launch round the Pool of London. That year also (1953) the school won first prize in the Wild Flower Show, before the 1975 Act of Parliament that now protects so many species and meant such competitions were unlawful and, therefore, abandoned.

Infectious diseases still spread through the school, and besides the usual mumps, chicken-pox etc., an epidemic of polio delayed opening of Island schools in September 1950. Playground accidents continued to bring cuts and bruises mainly due to its rough surface. Great sadness appeared, too, as on 5 January 1950 Mrs Wood (Green) wrote "With sorrow I record the death of Ronald Chopping (aged 9) on Christmas Eve." The little boy had suffered a ruptured appendix.

Mrs Green remained at the school just long enough to see the beginning of the reconstruction that was to bring it up to the standard now enjoyed. Her entry in the log dated 27 May 1960 says "Westridge Construction Ltd started building operations", and she left at the end of that summer term. The work continued for 9 months and lessons took place under great difficulties.

CHAPTER 13

Modernisation at last

A large extension and major refurbishment is never thought of today and done tomorrow, especially where local authorities are concerned. So it was with the reconstruction of Chale school. Perhaps the very beginning was the surfacing of the rough playground. The County Architect first inspected it in March 1948, agreed it needed doing badly, and thought it would be done that year. (He emphasised at the same time that the school was not on the list for interior redecoration at Easter.) True to his word, the work was completed in July 1948. Surprisingly the interior was decorated throughout also, perhaps the Architect had been appalled by what he found on his original visit, and pressed for action.

For the next 10 years the repairs that had to be done indicated the general state of the building. In 1949 the boiler received attention. The next thing to fail was the electricity, and in November, 1950, the school was rewired. Soon after that someone came to inspect the toilets and that led to the construction of a modern septic tank system. Any hope of comprehensive modernisation seemed to be lost when one Saturday in November, 1951, the Works & Buildings Sub-Committee visited (on a Saturday, mark you!) and decided against development.

After that came a stream of problems, inspections, and repairs - the fencing; the coal shed; a window; in spring 1952 a survey of the entire building for improvements and repairs; a new boiler pipe; the playground shelter in a dangerous condition (the head teacher said she had been reporting this since she arrived, and added "Mr Mew and Mr Roberts are the only Trustees of this decayed building and of the playground"). More interior decorations were done, but one day one of the Tortoise stoves refused to burn "smothering the new decorations in smoke and soot". New equipment was installed in the canteen, which had been created using part of the large mixed classroom. More consultations were held re the playground; the heating system again gave trouble; alterations were made to separate the boiler house and the cloakroom in summer 1956; more inspections of lavatories and electrical system; and dry rot damage appeared in 1957.

A spark of hope crept in during September of that year. The Deputy County Architect called and "glanced round school for possible building estimates". Another glimmer appeared in November when someone came "to look at the W.I. Hall with a view to renting for Infants" (presumably while major building went on). The following year the County Clerk of Works visited, meanwhile the stove in the Infants' Room was giving trouble. The medical officer was very concerned about its effect on health and a heating engineer was sent to inspect it.

Perhaps hope of comprehensive improvements died again in the autumn when the outside of the school was painted, and new wash basins were installed (why do that if bigger works were in the offing?). Then suddenly in December 1958 "Plans for proposed extensions arrived and appeared to Mrs Green to be almost totally unacceptable". Now, in spite of Mrs Green's reaction, things really began to move. Various men connected with County Hall Architect's Dept., the Surveyor, and builders arrived and inspected, measured and discussed throughout 1959. Eventually, in February the following year, representatives from Portsmouth Diocese Education Committee came to "visit the site of the new building and to discuss future disposition of house etc." At last modernisation was to be a reality.

Naturally much disruption of accommodation occurred. It was still possible for school to continue in the small classroom on the south of the building, and this is where the senior children had their lessons. All the other children attended at the Scout Hut (the W.I. Hall must have been unsuitable). Even so, many improvements were needed at the Scout Hut (to the kitchen, to heating, to toilets) to meet with LEA requirements. On 10 June it took all day for Infant and Middle Junior equipment to be transferred there. The head teacher, staff and cooks with the aid of a team of school-meals van drivers worked from 9 a.m. to 5.45 p.m.

All was ready for the younger children, but lack of sanitation at the school meant the older ones could not attend there. So they had 2 unexpected holidays, no mention is made of the solution to the problem, but apparently they were soon back at their desks. Perhaps everyone was glad to leave the turmoil a few days later when there was an outing to Hampton Court and school was closed while 26 children and 24 adults went off to enjoy the Palace, a river trip to Chertsey and tea at the Jolly Boatman.

It was Mrs Green's last term and, on 15 July 1960, she was presented with "a piece of furniture". She and Mr Green then gave a silver cup to the Secretary of Chale Horticultural Society (Mr E Snow) for competition by the children at the Annual Show. She left at the end of the month, and was succeeded the following September by Mr L Toms (who stayed just over 2 years).

For the next 8 months Mr Toms had a balancing act to perform in running the school at two locations. No pupil with a clear memory of those days has come forward, perhaps because it was the very youngest who were most involved, and maybe they thought all schools were so organised. The log book recorded very little, apart from the nuisance when the bus driver drove on past the Scout Hut, so the children had to walk back along the road. The entry to the Hut was also very inconvenient, being at that time down steps and straight on to a blind corner. Playtimes were difficult to deal with as there was very little space for outdoor activities.

Somehow everyone managed but it must have been with sighs of relief all round that the school moved back to the refurbished premises. The log entry reads simply "21 Feb. (1961) School reopened in new buildings." For the next 6 months, however, various small cracks, leaks, and adjustments needed attention. Slowly furnishings arrived, chairs for the hall came in March, and new curtains were fixed throughout the school in April. During the summer term the playground was re-instated, removing the last of the builders' rubbish and laying a new surface. When school opened in September that and the field were completed. This is the first mention of the field which adjoins the playground and was purchased from Mr   T. Roberts of Denhams Farm.

The latter part of the 20th century finally saw Chale C.of E. Controlled Primary School brought up to standard. At last they had a large assembly hall, a brand new Junior Classroom, efficient heating, and, perhaps best of all, modern toilet facilities with no longer the need for a dash across the playground in all weathers. Plans show that provision was made for an extra classroom to be built on the left of the main entrance. Thirty-five years later this has not been added. With no further housing development envisaged, and with the coming of Middle Schools in 1970/71 (see page 83) numbers on roll seem unlikely to need it.

Mr Toms recorded on his arrival that the school was divided into 3 parts: Juniors (which he taught), Middle Junior (Mrs Cox part-time) and Infants (Miss Rees). The last two classes were meeting in the Scout Hut. Morning assembly had to be a combined affair in the Hut, so that all children were under supervision should Miss Rees be late. She apparently lived at Brighstone, but how she travelled to work, and why she might be late is not mentioned. After assembly the older pupils then had to walk along the narrow road to their classroom. At lunch time the top class walked to the Scout Hut for dinner, each carrying a chair. If it was raining they held the chairs over their heads! A year later, in September 1961, the school became a "two class affair", and the number on roll was 53, 30 boys and 23 girls, up to the age of ll.

CHAPTER 14

Mr Ecclestone – Headmaster

Mr Wilfred Eccleston arrived in Chale on 1st May 1963. He was, as he put it, "Emergency trained", i.e. one of those who took the one year training course after his war service (see page 73). He taught in the North of England and in Somerset, before coming to Chale for what he later called the happiest 15 years of his teaching career. The number on roll was around 60 children up to the age of 11. Miss Rees was in charge of infants, and Mrs W Elems filled the post of part-time supply teacher.

Both Mr Eccleston's parents were teachers, and, like them, he was a born teacher. He must also have been one of the last traditional village schoolmasters in that he and his wife lived in the School House. He gave to the community much more than the teaching of their children in school hours.

The child's needs were to him paramount. He believed in providing his pupils with the basic tools of reading, writing and arithmetic, and beyond that he encouraged them to express themselves, through writing, speech, and drama. He was an accomplished self-taught guitarist, which, of course, meant daily assemblies always included music. The children's physical development was not neglected. Football matches against other primary schools, and Sports Days were a feature of every school year.

In Mr Eccleston's time, too, swimming came back on the timetable. No covered, heated public pool was yet available on the Island, so with the co-operation of parents, children were loaded into cars several times a week in the summer term and taken to Brighstone and/or Atherfield Holiday Camp. By special arrangement they used either Brighstone's indoor swimming pool, or Atherfield's outdoor one which was protected by a high glass surround. This must have required much dedication on the part of all concerned as Brighstone lessons took place between 8.30 a.m. and 9.30 a.m. while holiday camp guests were at breakfast, and teaching was at lunchtime at Atherfield. The high success rate (under the able tuition of Mrs V Sice [later Yull] and others) and the proud boast that all Chale children could swim, was the reward. In other years tuition took place at Niton's school pool, though unfortunately this was often disrupted by adverse weather or breakdown of the heating system.

A change in style in the log books gave a clue to another aspect of Mr Eccleston's character. On his second day he lists various repairs required and drew the attention of the Architectural Department's representative to "the alarming vibratory behaviour of the heating apparatus". Following the school's first "pet week" he listed various fauna brought to school and said "As the caretaker is still with us we can assume it has passed safely. It has not been a dull week." He also

81

noted "for the interest of future readers" that the gross amount of the allowance for the year was £135.

In this vein he continues throughout his years at Chale, managing to inject much humour into his reporting. Reading between lines his true summing up of any situation is obvious, yet he does not break the rules which say log books must not contain any personal opinions.

Mr Eccleston tried to involve all the local people in the school. Whether or not they were parents he sought to bring everyone into the building for a variety of events. To this end the Chale School Association was formed rather than a Parent/Teacher Association, and membership listed many who did not have children attending school. In the absence of a Village Hall, Mr Eccleston wanted the school to be used as a community centre. In this aim he was certainly very successful and soon Keep-Fit classes, Badminton sessions and Horticultural Shows among other activities took place in the school hall.

School outings to the mainland always included parents and friends, with 2 or 3 coaches needed for transport. Many also remember the Chale Pantomimes produced with Mr Eccleston's help during these years. They were extremely successful from 1968 and brought in badly needed funds to buy equipment and to help finance days out and parties. The venture came into being as the parents enjoyed the concerts given by the children and suggested they gave one for them, then it became a joint show. At that time several theatrically talented people lived in the village. Some wrote the script, others were good at singing, and others had an aptitude for acting and comedy (Noel Greville was an hilarious dame for several productions). After a year or two the school hall was not large enough to hold all those who wanted to attend so the performances moved to the hall at Atherfield Holiday Camp.

The delivery of a second-hand duplicator in May 1966 prompted another of Mr Eccleston's ideas for keeping people informed of events. He produced Chale School Magazine, called "The New Link" and he included drawings, poems and other writing by the children. When the Queen's Silver Jubilee was celebrated in 1977, Mr Eccleston took a leading role in arranging the festivities, and training the children for their part. It was indeed a great event[xx] with games, dancing, barbecue and bonfire, marred only by the perversity of English weather.

Mr & Mrs Eccleston loved living in the schoolhouse, and during their tenure the garden was a picture. Mr Eccleston's Albertine roses in massed bloom on the Junior Classroom wall were a delight, and shrubs and trees planted by him continue to flourish. With several false starts and skirmishes with C.C. ground staff (who seemed determined to mow small trees as well as grass), he eventually instituted the tree growing project. Some of the saplings were from seeds sown in the classrooms,

---

[xx] See separate booklet "Chale Celebrates"

others were provided by the Council. Miss Gallop's copse is the result and now adds interest to the playground.

Mrs Eccleston was a most valuable assistant to her husband and eventually became the official secretary and ancillary. But she put in far more hours in a voluntary capacity. She coached children who perhaps had missed school through illness, or who needed help with a particular problem. Mr Eccleston would set out a programme of individual teaching for the child and often she spent all day helping one pupil. The children all loved her, Mr Eccleston referred to her as a "surrogate mother" to them. The little ones especially used to run up to her in the morning for a cuddle and to say "I do love you".

So Mr Eccleston's reign continued through the '60s and into the '70s. With a firm and kindly hand he drew out the potential of his pupils. He brought people in to talk to the children on various subjects, just as his predecessors had done. One of the regular visitors was P.C. Dave Gurd, the last in another traditional post - that of village policeman, who lived in the Police House at the end of The Terrace. Miss Janet Gallop joined the staff when Mrs Spaven left in 1968, and was to prove a treasure and a mainstay of the school for many years and under three head teachers.

It may sound as if Mr Eccleston never put a foot wrong, however, now and then he upset individuals. Quite a storm broke out when he put election posters in the windows of his house. Occasionally, too, an item in The New Link did not please everyone. He was after all only human, and his sense of humour triumphed when looking back and he could smile over these incidents.

Meanwhile changes were going on at County and National level. The Isle of Wight was one of the first authorities to create Middle Schools. Partial re-organisation occurred in Autumn of 1970, the Junior age range then being 7 to 10 years. The next year plans were fully implemented, and all children over 9 years left to continue their education elsewhere. In Chale this meant travelling the 6 miles to Ventnor, and reduced the number on roll to 34 in 1971, as 14 children moved on. It grieved Mr Eccleston as he had always felt that the 10 and 11 year olds were the harvest of his years of teaching! ("Well, I would wouldn't I?" he said.) And he was very proud of the beautiful work "his" children produced at that age.

Another result of this decision was the closing of many small schools deemed uneconomic as numbers declined. In 1973 Mr Eccleston was summoned to County Hall and told the axe was to fall in Chale. The school was to be closed in September 1974. As the news spread through the parish, the whole village rose in protest. A public meeting was held on 10 April 1973, attended by over 100 people, from which two things emerged that helped ward off closure.

In the first place village residents determined to have a greater say at County level, and to that end one parent, Mrs Vera Sice, offered to put her name forward for the imminent elections. How imminent she did not realise until on her return home at midnight she told her husband who said "You'll have to hurry. Nominations are due in tomorrow at 12 noon."! She made it with only minutes to spare, having filled in forms, collected signatures and driven into Newport with a police escort of PC Gurd on his motorbike. On polling day she won a resounding victory and went on to serve on the Education Committee, and in many ways further the interests of Chale and its school.

The other outcome took longer. For some time there had been concern about the lack of housing for young people in the village. Those born and brought up locally found it impossible to rent a home of their own in Chale when they married and began to raise a family - potential pupils for the school. They had to move away, thus contributing to the decline in numbers on roll.

The Parish Council stepped in, producing a questionnaire circulated round the village, to find out how many houses for rent at a reasonable rate were needed. The answer appeared to be 12, and it is here the situation becomes very complicated. Suffice it to say the only land available within the village development plan was 4½ acres at the Green (now Spanners Close)[xxi]. The land was owned by the Church, and made up part of the glebe of Wootton parish (yet another complicated issue). The purchase had to be agreed, and though the need was for only part of this acreage, the whole packet of land had to be bought. The question of finance posed further problems, and various grants necessary for the project required certain conditions to be filled. In the end in order to get any housing at all many more than the dozen envisaged, and a wider variety of dwellings, had to be built.

On publication of the plans various objections were put forward, but Chale village was caught in a dilemma. Should they accept the project as proposed or lose their school? Finally the estate of mixed houses as seen today was built and is now managed by a housing association. Many Chale people feel it was a decision taken out of their hands, though they were promised that 50% of occupancy would be held for the locals, which was at least a compromise on the requirement. With the number of family homes included, it was hoped that the survival of the school was assured. The actual outcome of the building of the Spanners Close Estate must, however, be left to others to record. For the next 5 years or so, while work was in progress, the numbers at Chale School hovered around 30 to 40. Everyone's hopes were pinned on an influx of children when people began moving in.

Meanwhile days came and went much as before in the classroom. Mrs Judith Slade was appointed as part-time teacher in May 1975, and she came each morning to teach the very youngest in the reception class. The Managers recorded at their October meeting in 1975 that the hall curtains were in dire need of replacement. A year passed, however, before funds were allocated and the hall measured for them.

Financial difficulties at County level were repeatedly blamed around this time for postponement of repairs and replacements. Schools were not then in charge of their own budget, the managers merely asking for new items, or work to be done,

---

[xxi] This field being named after a Chale family eminent in the village in the 19th and early 20th centuries.

and these were attended to (or not) by the LEA. Neither were Managers responsible for agreeing and putting into practice policies on all aspects of management.

The seventies in small rural primary schools were perhaps the last years when managers were figureheads only. One local person involved at the time even said "Being a School Manager was a non-event". He said they mostly reported what was going on, kept an eye on the building, equipment and fitments, and said who could or could not hire the hall. Organisers of any events concerned with the Church, or uniformed youth groups had free use of the building, paying only for lighting and heating. Some regular users were even school key holders.

Educational changes were not far off, and began in Chale with the retirement at the end of the autumn term, 1977, of Mrs Eccleston as school secretary. A presentation was made at a crowded school concert attended by over 100 parents. Mr Eccleston's report to the Managers states (or understates) that she leaves "after many years serving the school in various capacities. She will be greatly missed by staff and children." Her job then became a shared one between Mrs Brookes and Mrs Pauline Chiverton. Another presentation was made at the same time, when the Chale Jubilee Committee gave the village an ornamental striking clock, bought with funds left over from that celebration. The Headmaster's report for March, 1978, records that "The clock is to hang in the School Hall until such time as a better alternative location is available". It is still there today (1996).

After Easter the following year, another blow fell, when the Chairman (Rev. N. Ward) reported to the Managers that the Head Teacher would be retiring at the end of the academic year. Sad as everyone must have been by this news, steps had to be taken immediately to advertise for and appoint a replacement. At a meeting on 31 May 1978 names were put forward for representatives of the Managing Body to serve on both the shortlisting panel and the appointment panel.

Mr Eccleston's last entry in the log book reads "School closed for Summer Holidays, one day early because tomorrow is I.W. Agricultural Show. I ended my teaching career today, after 15 years as Headmaster of this School. Ten children move on to Middle School in September. New Term starts September 5th". And the Managers' Minutes record that they "wished to place on record their warmest thanks and appreciation for the excellent contribution that Mr Eccleston has made to ensuring the success of the school during his many years as Headmaster". The summer holidays began, and the village awaited the arrival of the new headteacher.

CHAPTER 15

Mrs. Sporne's Time

When the advertisement for Mr Eccleston's successor was placed Chale expected to have another male teacher. However, from a short list of 6 applicants, and under the direction of the local Education Committee, the post went to the one woman interviewed, Mrs J Sporne. Several good reasons influenced this choice. For one thing Mrs Sporne was well qualified, for another it seemed likely that she intended it to be a long term situation. The interviewing panel felt that for the male applicants a small rural school was just a stepping stone in a career aimed at progression to a larger urban school. In addition Mrs Sporne was a member of the Church of England (as was her predecessor) and indicated her willingness to live in the school house and become part of the local community.

In the end Mrs Sporne became the first Chale head teacher who did not live on the premises. A change of policy on the part of the LEA meant the rent was raised to an unacceptable level (for Mr Eccleston it had been only nominal). In addition she already had a modern home of her own, and the disruption of domestic arrangements to take up residence in what by then had become an old-fashioned and inconvenient smaller house was not attractive. Nationwide few headteachers of small rural schools (or even any day schools) were then living on the job in a tied house. Consequently Mrs Sporne was not often present at village events and this was a great disappointment to many local residents. The school house did not stand empty as the caretaker, Chris Barton, made it his home from 1979 until the 1990s. Certainly it was most helpful to have the house occupied by someone so closely concerned with the care of the school.

Initially Mrs Sporne made several changes. She brought in new reading and science books and introduced gymnastics, woodwork, and natural sciences. Gardening lessons were continued though were short-lived owing to cut-backs on work by ground-staff. Nevertheless in later years with her encouragement Chale's chequerboard garden was successfully completed.

Mrs Sporne requested the use of the "annexe" on the south side of the school house as a music room. This referred to the former boys' schoolroom. It had not been used for some years, possibly because it was damp, inconvenient and not heated by the school central heating system. Unfortunately, this was another short-lived scheme as the cold and damp persisted and adversely affected the equipment.

One happy outcome did result, however, when Mrs Sporne inspected the room. She found the First World War Memorial plaque hidden away, leaning against a wall in the small store room. Possibly it was put there for safety during the renovations in 1960, and with various changes of head teacher had been forgotten. The inscription states that this memorial should be hung in the school as an ever-present reminder of the terrible years when Chale's former school children left the village to serve their country, many of them never to return. Mrs Sporne arranged immediately for the board to be cleaned and put up in the school hall. Happily the lettering had not deteriorated during its long stay in the dark and damp. This find then initiated a search for the board listing pupils successful in the pre-war scholarship examination (which Mrs Sporne had been told about), but this did not come to light.

From the summer of 1981, with the headteacher's and the LEA's permission, the room became the venue for the Playgroup run by Mrs Wendy Barney (later Bremner) on 3 mornings each week. Modern electric heaters were installed and eventually a toilet cubicle was added. When Mrs Barney moved to teach Chale's Juniors part-time, Mrs Anne Moss took over, and after her Mrs Anita Cotton. Then in 1991 Wendy took charge once more.

With enthusiasm Mrs Sporne undertook the necessary updating of the school brochure. Later she introduced a new uniform (green sweat shirts with logo, and track suit bottoms). There were still only 30 or so on roll, but building work at the Green had started and an influx of children was expected in the not-too-distant future.

Following the passing of the 1980 Education Act the managers had a name change. They became governors, and this was the beginning of far-reaching changes in that decade. For one thing, in the spring of 1981, conditions for hire of the hall were changed, which meant that charges rose considerably, to cover costs formerly borne by the LEA. This caused much disappointment among local organisations which now found they could not afford to hire the building. Chale Horticultural Society's Autumn Show had to be held in the W.I. Hall which was smaller and less convenient than the school. Keep-fit classes were discontinued as hall hire charges meant fees had to be raised to an unacceptable level. So the community lost another contact with the school.

At County level cut-backs in funding and postponement of repairs etc. became a regular feature in the Headteachers' report. So also were lists of in-service courses Chale's teachers were required to attend. These had long been a feature of school life, but now there seemed to be more and more. Mrs Sporne joined in discussions re curriculum development in music, art/craft, science, and P.E., and was also a member of the History/Geography study group which met regularly. Miss Gallop went to First Aid, among others.

Mrs Sporne's log book entries listed a stream of visitors, which must have been a constant interruption to her duties both as teacher and administrator of the school. These included the LEA English Co-Ordinator, County Chief Engineer, Senior Reading Adviser, Safety Officer, and the Senior Psychologist, all of course needing the headteacher's time and full attention. It is easy to see that she lead a very busy life, and the load of office work for her and for those employed in similar positions in other schools became very heavy. This especially affected schools too small to be able to afford more than a few hours part-time secretarial assistance or additional teaching staff to cover lessons when the head was dealing with office work. By autumn 1980 the number on roll was still in decline, there being only 27 children. This improved slightly as the term went on, and hopes were pinned on families taking up residence at Chale Green. After half-term 10 children were admitted from the new development, bringing numbers on roll to 44, with others to come after Easter. At last the effect of the new estate was beginning to benefit Chale school.

In rural areas all over the country teachers and parents were finding problems arising entirely due to small pupil numbers. For one thing the increasing use of computers (Chale received its first in 1984) required skills not everyone had, and this meant attending more in-service courses. Then cut-backs on peripatetic music teachers meant that side of school work was squeezed into perhaps no more than an hour or so a week. The difficulty of teaching sports, art, woodwork and other specialist skills brought more problems. In addition, for many children the move from primary to middle or secondary school was quite stressful as they found themselves amongst a crowd of total strangers, as only one or two from their school had moved on at the same time. In this context, and in common with similar schools in other counties, the Wight Association of Small Primary Schools (WASPS) was set up in 1987. Mrs Sporne was a leading light in this and for the year 1988/89 she acted as co-ordinator. At the time of writing 6 schools participate, involving 350 children and 21 teachers.

Such associations aimed to share special skills their individual teachers might have, bringing the children together for days of sport, music etc. They joined each other for educational trips and entertainment, and for the WASPS this also included a brief school "holiday" when they stayed locally altogether for 2 or 3 nights. The children then had the opportunity to get to know some of their age group from other schools, which meant more acquaintances and familiar faces when they left Chale. The greater numbers also enabled social skills of sharing and communication to be learnt, and accustomed pupils to being in crowded situations.

The present (1996) co-ordinator of WASPS says the group "strives to accomplish these enhancements (as above) whilst continuing to provide the advantages of being educated in a small school". It's a philosophy, she adds, to which all members are committed.

Towards the end of the 1980s even more problems arose. The Education Reform Act of 1988 brought in Local Management of Schools (LMS) when governors became responsible for many duties formerly undertaken by the LEA. School policies had to be formulated on many subjects (health & safety, smoking, truancy, sex education etc.), each school had to have a Constitution approved, and a school brochure which met specific conditions. Being governor of a school was no longer the "non-event" described formerly (see page 85). The LEA offered much support through various experts on their staff, but governors nevertheless had to take over the school's financial affairs, deal with staffing, create a school development plan and many other areas of administration. While these responsibilities had been taken from the schools in 1902 when Church schools had accepted management by the LEA (in exchange for help with funding), it now seemed that they were being given back...and much was additionally required.

At the same time the 1988 Act introduced the National Curriculum, with targets to be reached by certain age groups, and tests to be instituted. Much has been said for and against the system of requiring all state schools to follow the same course of studies. The aim was to give every child, whatever school he/she attended, and in whatever part of the country they lived, rural or urban, the same basic educational opportunities. As an ideal it is difficult to fault this, but in practice it was hard to administer. For small schools particularly, the result was yet another burden of work descending on just one or two teachers in each establishment. Across the country this caused much stress as people endeavoured to learn new ways and fit new requirements into already crowded schedules.

Governors, too, found many more than the obligatory 3 meetings per year (one a term) were now needed, so they had to create sub-committees to work between the termly meetings to present reports in due time. Courses for Governors were instituted by the LEA, and that, too, meant giving up leisure time to attend. Many felt they were battling through a fog and totally unable or unsuited to doing what was required of them.

In amongst all this the village benefited from Mrs Sporne's concern and kindness in several ways during the eighties. The shop and Post Office at Church Place, adjacent to the school, closed. The lack of this facility at that end of the parish created much inconvenience, especially for the older residents. As no other premises were available Mrs Sporne offered a small room in school for part-time use as a Post Office. Agreement was reached with the authorities, and were on 3 afternoons a week pensions, stamps and so on have been dispensed within Chale school, first by Joanna Barney, then (among others) Audrey Hardcastle and Rodney Archer[xxii]. When the mobile chiropody unit required a stopping place with electricity supply available, Mrs Sporne was approached. With her agreement, and the consent of the LEA, this also was arranged. The clinic then called one afternoon a month from the autumn of 1980.

From Mrs Twyman's day Chale school has provided an excellent mid-day meal for pupils. Briefly in the 1980s the modern kitchen (constructed during the 1960 renovations) became a "servery" only, meals being brought from Niton school. However, roles have now been reversed, and dinner is once more cooked in Chale's kitchen, some of the meals being sent to Niton[xxiii]. When this happened Mrs Sporne offered to supply mid-day meals to local residents. Originally this was to boost numbers, and it has proved popular. The greatest influx of village people being at Christmas. Nowadays it is not to receive Sir Henry's charity of bread for the "children and aged persons of Chale"(see page 7), but to enjoy Barbara Knapp's beautifully

---

[xxii] Unfortunately this has had to be discontinued owing to a break-in and burglary.
[xxiii] This also has been discontinued as Niton now has its own excellent kitchen.

cooked lunch of turkey and all the trimmings, followed by Christmas pudding and custard. In 1993 20 people joined the children and since then numbers have risen.

Mrs Sporne also made sure the children were present when the village car park was opened, and when trees (provided by a legacy for the purpose from Mr H. Cheek, late of Chale Manor) were planted in a field between Stroud Green and North Grounds. Encouraged by Mrs Sporne, the school children went on a sponsored walk up St Catherine's Down to the Hoy Monument in the summer of 1991. Part of the proceeds from this went towards the fund for the refurbishment of the Monument in June the following year.

So in spite of not living in Chale, she still managed to include the children in notable events and introduce changes and improvements that have helped the village.

This was the situation in which Mrs Sporne found herself, but that was not where her problems ended. At home she had domestic difficulties which also created stress. The many pressures began to tell and it is small wonder that her health gave way and she was off sick for some weeks in the summer of 1990, and again in spring of 1991.

These years were perhaps not the most successful for Chale School. Mrs Sporne's absence, and her replacement by various supply teachers, created a degree of dissatisfaction. Some children were confused by the many changes. Several parents took advantage of new regulations which allowed them to send their children to schools out of their home catchment area, so contributing to the decline in numbers down to just 24 in September 1992. Chale School Association suffered from lack of members, and was discontinued. In the wake of this came the necessity for fund raising to provide such traditional treats as the school Christmas Party. Perhaps relatively small considerations individually, but all adding to the pressures on the headteacher.

Another blow fell when Miss Gallop was taken ill and rushed to hospital for an operation in early 1993. To the Governors' dismay this brought a letter from the insurance company saying they were no longer prepared to finance the employment of supply teachers. The company felt the school was a poor risk as it had made so many calls on the policy recently. With the aid of the LMS adviser from the LEA, this emergency was dealt with, but things again looked very bleak when in the summer term Mrs Sporne was ill once more.

Nevertheless, a few gleams of light appeared here and there. Everyone was pleased to see Miss Gallop restored to health when she came back to school in the summer term. Behind the scenes, too, work was going on to organise the grand celebration of the school's 150 years in its present building. The local community became involved with the proposed festivities, a new spirit of optimism was generated, memories and memorabilia from the past were brought out, and help was offered (and gratefully accepted) from many quarters. Added to that a strong and supportive board of governors was gradually learning its role and putting much work, energy and enthusiasm into the task of restoring the school's fortunes.

Mrs Sporne was still unable to work at the beginning of the autumn term, 1993, and so missed the exciting (for the children) and nail-biting (for the Celebration Committee) run-up to the Great Day. As Victorian artefacts from Carisbrooke Castle and Chale Women's Institute arrived, and mementoes of the early nineteenth century came from former pupils, as the Chale School Celebration Book was published, and many photographs from long ago (and not so long ago) appeared, anticipation mounted.

The week before saw one wonderful day spent at the Havenstreet Steam Railway. All the children, staff and helpers dressed in period costume set off in a very up-to-date coach kindly provided by one of the parents. For some of the children it was a thrilling first ride on a steam train. Though late in the season there were still many holiday visitors about and the children behaved perfectly, providing the tourists with an added attraction on their trip. The County Press and Meridian TV were also in attendance, and the reward was a report in the paper and a brief - even 'fleeting'! - appearance on the local TV news.

The day was fast approaching, the Great Day, even the Actual Day, when 150 years previously the Churchwardens and Overseers had signed the original Deed of Trust for the establishment of Chale School in its new premises (see page 8). Hopes were high that in 1993, 25 September would be as momentous as it must have been in 1843. And so it proved!

CHAPTER 16

A Day to Remember

At last the planning was over. The flags were put out, the children were decked in Victorian clothes, the day had arrived. For a century and a half local children had been taught in the same building and celebrations were in order.

The Celebration Committee viewed the weather anxiously that morning. A cold wind swept the playground but happily it wasn't one of the Force 8 gales which are a regular feature of the South coast in spring and autumn. A hint of rain from the overcast sky threatened to upset the day. Everyone crossed fingers and hoped for the best.

Cheese, bread and pickles for ploughman's lunches were loaded on trestles in the marquee erected on the playing field. The furled Union Jack hung on the flag pole awaiting the colour party of Chale & Niton scouts to release it to signal commencement of proceedings. Rows of chairs were arranged on the playground for the opening ceremony and the children's performance. One hundred and fifty years of memorabilia was on view in the school hall, a book for signatures of those attending lay open, copies of Chale School Celebration Book were ready for purchasers, and a table groaned with raffle prizes.

Well-known village personalities stood at their posts - Edward Roberts, Derek Sprake, Bartons, Chivertons, Whittingtons - all names likely to have been found in the earliest registers. Members of Chale W.I., the C. of E. and Methodist Churches, the Charity Club and local businesses, all supported the venture - truly a community event.

Janet Gallop, Infants' teacher, was deputising for the headmistress, Josie Sporne, who through illness could only put in a token appearance. All the school staff, supply teacher, ancillary, cook, caretaker, lent a hand.

Computers had been tucked away and the Infants' room re-arranged with blackboard and old-fashioned desks, the dreaded cane to hand to simulate the original classroom. Everywhere, on walls, tables and cupboard tops, the school exhibited results of various Victorian projects undertaken in preparation for this day.

At 10 o'clock, from the tower of St Andrew's Church, Edwin Cole and his team of bellringers rang out the news that Chale was celebrating its school's long existence, and a banner on the church wall spread the message to those passing-by on the Military Road. Visitors started to pour into the school grounds, many dressed in Victorian costume for the occasion. Mabel Nicholson wore her grandmother's wedding dress, Mike Starke appeared in labourer's outfit, Andrew Burroughs sported a frock coat and top hat, others dressed as domestic servants. The scene and the atmosphere were set.

After colours were broken, the Rector (Jon Russell) said a prayer of thanksgiving. He introduced the official "opener", Mr R (Dick) Dabell. As everyone was feeling cold (except the Rector in his flowing black cloak) Dick kept his speech short. The Dabell family, he recalled, was closely linked with the school from its earliest days. In the same year the school was built his great-grandfather, Alexander Dabell, opened Blackgang Chine to the public. He put in a plea for the retention of small rural schools as a valued part of village life. He ended by presenting the school with a generous cheque for £150, £1 for every year of its existence.

Tessa Bloodworth, Diocesan Education Officer, came next, and presented the certificate from the National Society, signed by the Archbishop of Canterbury, which now hangs in the front hall. Dick Dabell cut the Celebration cake kindly made and decorated by John Woodford, chef at Blackgang, and the Opening Ceremony concluded. All of it (with other activities of the day) safely recorded on video by Mike Jackman.

The children, trained by Mike's wife, Jill, entertained with singing, dancing and recitation. Chale was the smallest school on the Island at that time and all 24 pupils performed, the girls in shining white pinafores, the boys in makeshift knickerbockers, shirts, kerchiefs and flat caps. Then hall and marquee were besieged as old pupils, present parents and friends met each other, in some cases for the first time in many years. An honoured octogenarian guest was 1930's headteacher, Mrs Twyman.

A reporter and photographer from the County Press interviewed our oldest former pupil, Mrs Dorothy Whittington aged 96, and some of the youngest present day children. In the Infants' room a class in Victorian days was re-enacted and caused much amusement, and shudders of terror as Janet Gallop, beloved and gentle teacher, turned into a fearsome martinet, reinforcing her words by striking the desk with a cane. Meanwhile on the playing field John Hardy kept the younger ones amused by organising old fashioned (but still popular) games, conkers, hopscotch, skipping, bowling a hoop. Wendy Hardy and helpers served umpteen lunches, and Norah and Susan Morey with their assistants dealt with afternoon tea drinkers.

The day passed swiftly, and all too soon for those who were busy reminiscing about past schooldays, the time came to leave. Fortunately the rain had held off, and at 5 o'clock the flag was lowered, the Rector said a closing prayer, and another peal of bells signalled the conclusion. Willing hands cleared the hall and made all ready for Monday's lessons.

So ended Chale School's Celebration Day, perhaps the village's biggest community effort since the Queen's Silver Jubilee in 1977.

CHAPTER 17

Into the 21st Century

The 1993 Celebrations marked a milestone in the life of Chale School, and a turning point in its history, but certainly not the end of its story. The years since then have seen many changes.

Mrs Sporne took early retirement at the end of the autumn term owing to ill health. Mrs Helen Flynn, was appointed early in 1994, and took up her post after Easter that year. She was much liked and so successful that the LEA asked her to move to another local school that needed help to improve its grades. Their gain was Chale's loss, but Mrs Sandy Nordbruch took over in January 1999, and has proved an excellent choice, so much so that for some months until July 2002 she was also in charge of Chillerton School.

In Mrs Sporne's time the school won a prize in the Village Ventures competition, run by the Rural Development Council and the Isle of Wight County Press, for the communal effort that led up to the 150th Anniversary Celebrations. Helen Flynn added to this by her encouragement which resulted in the village winning first prize in the same competition the following year, for the launching of the Wednesday evening Games Club for village families. This continues and caters for children to age 13. In 1995 as the 50th anniversary of VE Day was celebrated, the children prepared a book of war reminiscences contributed by local people, "Chale School Remembers", which won first prize in the National Charity Education Extra competition. Another success was achieved with their entry to the 1995 Wight in Bloom competition, and yet again in 2002 for the continuation of the Games Club

Sadly, the Post Office had to be closed in the later 1990s following a break-in. There have been changes in teaching staff. Janet Gallop retired in 1998, after 30 years' wonderful service, but everyone is pleased to see her on the occasional morning when she arrives to take Assembly. Carolyn Sutton joined the staff that autumn as Janet's replacement. Office staff also changed. In fact only two staff members continue with Chale School into the 21st century. Chris Barton is still the caretaker, though he has moved from the school house, and Barbara Knapp remains as cook.

The building itself has seen many changes. With the blessing of the LEA, the Governors have taken over the school house which has been altered to provide a staff room, a cookery room, a meeting room (for community use), and improvements to the pre-school area (renamed the Nursery). In 2002 a new computer room was added near the rear entrance. The back garden has been landscaped for easier maintenance. Chale Nursery's play area in front of the school building has been improved with new equipment and a safety surface. The roses previously there and the plaque in memory of Mrs B. Rogers, a former School Helper, have been moved to the rear.

An association called Friends of Chale School, under the leadership of John Hardy, now helps with the Wednesday Club, with various after-school clubs, and with fund-raising. Members (both parents and others) are always prepared to contribute in whatever way they can. Local residents continue to be invited into school to talk to the children on subjects on which they have special knowledge, or to demonstrate a particular skill. Various parents help with reading and craftwork in the classrooms. School lunches are enjoyed by many local people. The number of pupils still hovers around 40, but the thriving Chale Nursery suggests hope for the future.

And what about the original Charities? Well, they have been wound up. Diminishing returns on the investments, due to inflation, changes in the business world, and general social change, meant the annual income fell to about £10, and they had outgrown their usefulness. Then changes in Charity Law and requirements of the Charities Commission made it entirely uneconomic to continue, and the final meeting of Trustees took place in September 1994[xxiv]. The charities at that time were not run by the Rector and Churchwardens, but were in the hands of a Board of Trustees, consisting of local residents and including the Rector (who lives at Shorwell). Mr F Hollis, of Stroud Green Farm House, was the last Chairman. Since the 1902 Act, after which the dividends were no longer needed to pay the school master, the money had been allocated for various purposes. For many years £2 was set aside for needlework prizes one in each of the seven school grades plus one for the best Infant (5 shillings each) – girls only, of course. Money in excess of this provided books either for the school, or for the Sunday Schools at St. Andrews and the Methodist Church, Pupils who succeeded in passing the scholarship or 11+ exam. were also given a share to help with expenses for books, travelling or school clothing. A number of post-war pupils still living locally benefited in this way.

The ending of Chale's Charities meant the end of an era. At a meeting of Trustees on 30 March, 1994, it was recorded that "Mr Dabell expressed the view that the original benefactors, though saddened, would feel that the right decision had been taken" [94]. The people of the village do indeed owe a great debt to the donors' generosity. One thing that does remain, and was rescued from the clock tower of the Church for the school celebrations, is the large board now hanging in the entry hall of the school. This lists the donors, dates and amounts of the charities (was it another item stored away in 1960 when the school was extended?). Ken Morey manhandled it down from the tower, cleaned it of the dust of many years and polished up the brass lettering. The photograph of Sir Henry Worsley, taken from a bust of him at the

[xxiv] These Charities are not to be confused with Chale Charity Club (founded by a few local residents) which for some years did extremely good work in raising money for Island charities.

Royal Asiatic Society's headquarters in London (and also now hanging in the entry hall), was presented in 1996.

Closure scares brought worries in late 1993, and again in 1996, happily these were weathered. As for the village itself, the changes are numerous. Though the area remains agricultural modern methods mean that very few men are employed on farms. While some people can only find part-time or seasonal work (at Blackgang Theme Park, the Wight Mouse or farther afield), others are unfortunately unemployed. Poverty still exists but not in the abject condition of 200 years ago. Nowadays there is no need to record that the children have no boots to wear so cannot go to school (see page 15). Car ownership, too, enables people of the village to travel farther afield for a wider range of employment and leisure opportunities.

The Church does not have the authority it once had but staff and others connected with the school have always sought to raise children in the Christian tradition. Chale now shares its parish priest with Shorwell and Gatcombe, and religion is not the firm base of society that it once was. Nevertheless, the ideals of the Church of England are still at the heart of the school just as they were when it became part of the National Society for the Promotion of the Education of the Poor in the Principles of the Established Church in 1843.

This story is not unique, it echoes that of countless rural schools in England and Wales. "Change and adapt" is perhaps the universal and on-going motto of them all. The problems, worries and heart-ache that followed the 1988 Education Reform Act are proof of this. Getting into the stride of new requirements has also given many people (especially those on governing boards) a deeper insight into our education system.

Chale School has moved from Charity School, to Parochial Schools, to Voluntary (or Non-Provided) School, to Voluntary Controlled C. of E. School, and from the only school for children until they went out into the world at age 14, to Primary School up to the age of 11, and now catering for children just to age 9, and nowadays officially termed a C. of E. Controlled Primary School. The children are better fed, better clothed, better housed, healthier and brighter. The original, overcrowded and unhygienic buildings have become spacious, light and modern with all the up-to-date equipment required and expected in a new century. The WASPS (see page 88) continues (Sandy Nordbruch was Co-ordinator until July 2002), helping the pupils to expand horizons. They have been introduced to overseas travel and have links with schools in Sweden, Finland, Germany and Italy. Some members of staff have visited teachers in these countries to exchange information and ideas. At the heart of it, there always remains the aim to give the children a good start in life, and to introduce them to a wider world so they can develop to their full potential.

Will 2043 see another generation of children spending their first schooldays in the building at the foot of St Catherine's Down, just as many have before them? Will they play round the matured trees of Miss Gallop's copse, hear Bible stories at daily assembly and make visits at Christmas and Easter to the Church? By the Grace of God they will. To-day's village hopes that to-morrow's community will celebrate the 200th Anniversary of the school's foundation in these premises with as much enjoyment as they had in 1993.

Finally, how did it happen that such a small, poor and remote place had a school so early in education history? One reason for its early establishment and on-going success was put forward by a present-day resident already mentioned, a former pupil and a well-known character, Edward Roberts. When asked his opinion he said simply "We had the Worsleys!"

Appendix 1
Chale School Head Teachers

Date	Name
May 1608	- English (unlicensed)
Feb. 1800	Mr. William Dash
Jan. 1806	Mr. John Margetts, tenant Goodalls, no definite evidence that he was school - master but highly likely., J. Margetts was buried at Chale 9.7.1837, aged 69.
1841	Mr. James Grapes.
Sep. 1843	Mr. Abraham Baker.
Sep. 1870	Mr. James Bryant.
1875	Mr. William Pratt.
Mar. 1879	Mr. Henry (Harry) Flint.
1879	Mr. Frederick Guy (Listed as Certificated Master in directory dated 1879, IWRO, 914/ISL/1879, no other information except Mr Flint rumoured to have died in office.)
Oct. 1882	Mr. George Amos.
Aug. 1891	Mr. John Cooke.
Sep. 1922	Mr. J. Cooke retires aged 60.
Oct. 1922	Mrs. E. Z. Cooke
Nov. 1924	Above retires after 33 yrs service, was former infant teacher.
Dec. 1924	Miss Marjorie C. Pike.
Mar. 1927	Miss O. W. Whitehouse.
Oct. 1928	Miss V. A. Martin.
Jan. 1936	Miss Lucy M. Jennings.
Mar. 1936	Mr. George R. J. Gutteridge.
Apr. 1936	Miss Esther A. Loosemore.
Feb. 1945	Above referred to as Mrs Twyman for first time.
Dec. 1945	Mrs Twyman granted leave of absence (maternity).
Sep. 1946	Mrs Twyman took up duties again.
Jan. 1948	Mrs Margaret E. Drudge.
Apr. 1948	Mrs. W. A. Wood.
Jun. 1954	Mrs Wood married Mr Green.
Sep. 1960	Mr L. Toms.
Jan. 1963	Mr Wellesley C. Elems.
May 1963	Mr Wilfred Eccleston.
Sep. 1978	Mrs J. Sporne.
Apr. 1994	Mrs. Nordbruch

(Full list of Staff from 1902 to be found in Log Book dated from Autumn Term, 1966, under 'S'; and of Managers under 'M')

Appendix 2

SPECIFICATION
of Works to be done in Erecting a School at
Chale Isle of Wight for the Rev.d A.W.Gother

<u>Mason Etc.</u>

Excavate the ground under all walls etc. of a sufficient depth for a good foundation.
Build good rubble walls with Brick Quoins colo(u)red to match walls of the heights
and thicknesses shown on drawings and Good Grey Lime mortar.
Shafts of Chimneys and part of Flues to be of Brick colo(u)red to match walls.
All the Stones to be delivered on the ground by the Rev(eren)d
A W Gother free of any expense to the Builder.
Put slates all round on walls to keep down damp.
Cover the Roofs with best Duchess or Countess slates with zinc nails.
The ridge to be covered with glazed Ridge Tiles.
The floors of Porch, Scullery and Pantry to be laid with smooth paving and also the
Boys' Privy.
Put 3 Purbeck Steps to Doors.
Smooth paving hearth Stone to all Fire places.
Put cement chimney pots to all the Flues.
Run cement Tablet in Front for an inscription.
Plaster with 2 C(oa)t Rendering the walls of Schoolrooms Living Room and
Chambers.
All the ceilings to be 3 C(oa)t Lath and plaster.
Lime white the walls of Scullery, Pantry and Privies.
Build 4½ Brick partition between Pantry and Scullery.
Build Small Oven with iron Door.
9 Yards of Pitching with rough stones in Back Yard.

<u>CARPENTER</u>

All Timbers to be of the sizes shown on drawings.
The joist and bond to Chamber floors Lintels and Timbers of all the Roofs to be of
the Best Red Pine.
Roofs to be Battened with 3/4 yellow Pine Battens
2 1/4 x 3/4.
Put 2 Oak Rustic Posts to carry Veranda.

| Boy's | Put 1 Red Deal floor, Oak joist 4 x 2½ sleepers |
| School Room | 4 x 1 1/4. Red Deal Rabt.(rebated) and champd. (chamfered) |

Door case 5 1/4 x 3 doweled with Iron dowels into stone step. 1 3/4 stiles to Door 1 rails fram(e)d in Do. filled in flush with 3/4 tong(ue)d Battens, champ(fere)d) window frames 4½ x 3 with oak projecting sills 1 bevelled skirting 10 in. wide with one iron casement to open in each window. One Louvre Ventilator with shutter in inside. Two 7/8 round Iron bolts and nuts to tie in plate.

Girl's To be finished the same as Boys' School.

Living Room Floor, joist, Door, Door base, and window frame etc. to be the same as School Rooms, 3/4 square skirting 5 wide, 1 Wt. Deal steps and risers to stairs with 1 1/4 string. One Cupboard under enclosed with 3/4 Wt. deal match and beaded boarding - no door allowed at foot of Stairs

1 1/4 4 panel door with Door case 3½ x 2½ between Scullery and Living Room hung with 3 in. butts 6 in. rim lock, 1 window board 18 ft. Supl., 1 Am shelves to Cup-board, Dead Closet Lock to Cupboard Door. Brass Button and knob / hung with 12 X garnetts.

Scullery Put Red Deal Door case 3½ x 2½ doweled into stone sill. 1 Ledg(e)d Door hung with 14 X garnetts 6 in. round bolt and Thumb Latch, Window frame 3½ x 2½ with end casement hung - 1 window board.

Pantry Red Deal Door case 3½ x 2½ doweled into stone, 3/4 ledged Door hung with 12 garnetts. Thumb latch, 7 in. fine plate lock, Window frame and board same as Scullery with half-glass and half zinc, 36 ft of 1 shelves.

Wood House Red Deal Door case 3½ x 2½ doweled into stone. 3/4 ledged Door and fastening same as Pantry.

Privies Red Deal Door case 3/4 ledged Door and 1 seat and riser. Deal floor to the Girls Privy.

East Chamber 1 Spruce floor, 3/4 square skirting 5 wide 1 window board. 4 quarter partition to enclose stairs and to form closet. 1 1/4 square framed pan(e)l Door to D(itt)o. & Closet, 1½ rabbtd (rebated) jambs, 7/8 mo(u)lding round D(itt)o 4 ft of 1 shelf and Pin rail. 6in. iron rim lock to Door, Spring latch to Closet D(itt)o, window frame etc same as below.

Chamber Floor, Skirting, Window and Door same as last described.

Chamber Floor, Window and Door same as last, 3/4 Skirting 4 1/4 wide.

Put iron bolt through and proper bridging to joists over Living Room. Plain wood chim(ne)y pieces to all Fire places.

Painter, Plumber and Glazier

Paint all the outside 4 Coats oil in plain colo(u)r.
All the inside 3 C(oa)ts D(itt)o.
Glaze the windows as per plan and cement lights.
Put Lead Gutters behind chimneys and flashing to D(itt)o. Lead flashings to Roofs of
Schools by side of House. Lead over Porch of 4 lbs. to the foot. Lead Gutter to Roof
and 2 Valleys of 5 lb(s) to the foot Superficial.

16 March 1843   W.Way & Son
                                Builders, Newport I.W

BIBLIOGRAPHY

BARNARD H.C.,	A history of English Education from 1760, 2nd Edition, Uni. of London Press, 1961.
CASTLE, E.B.	A Parents' Guide to Education, Penguin, 1968
HASSELL, J.	A Tour of the Isle of Wight, I.o.W., 1790.
H.M.S.O.	Primary Education, 1959, reprinted 1960.
HORN, Pamela	Education in Rural England 1800-1914, Gill & MacMillan Ltd, Dublin, 1978.
HORN, Pamela	The Victorian & Edwardian Schoolchild, Alan Sutton, Gloucester, 1989.
HORN, Pamela	The Victorian Country Child, Alan Sutton, Gloucester, 1990.
KINGSWELL, Peter	Fidelity Will Haunt Me Till I Die, Privately published by the Royal Marines Historical Society, 1991.
LANCASTER, Joseph	Improvements in Education, 3rd Ed., Darton & Harvey, 1805, Reprinted Augustus M. Kelley, U.S.A., 1973.
LEWIS, June R.	The Village School, Robert Hale, 1989.
LOWNDES, G.A.N.	The Silent Social Revolution, O.U.P.,1969
MIDDLETON, N. & WEITZMAN, S.	A Place for Everyone, Gollancz Ltd, 1976.
MINISTRY OF EDUCATION,	A Guide to the Educational System of England & Wales, Pamphlet No.2, H.M.S.O.,1945, (Reprinted 1947)
MORRISH, I.	Education since 1800, Allen & Unwin, 1970.
RAE, J	Too Little Too Late?, Collins, 1989.
SHORT, B. (Ed.)	The English Rural Community, Image & Analysis,C.U.P., 1992.
SMITH,	F.A History of English Elementary Education 1760 – 1902, Uni. of London Press, 1931
TIRRELL,L.B.	The Aided Schools Handbook, A. R. Mowbray & Co., 1956.
VENABLES, Rev. E.A.	A Guide to the Isle of Wight, London, 1860

References

1   Hants. Miscellany II, Portsmouth Public Library 262.9 P.87, D/1/C Licenses of Schoolmasters & Lecturers

2   Hants. R.O., Chale Visitation Returns 1788, 21M65 B4/3/170

3   Janet Darney's Story, by Sarah Doudney, Pub. Religious Tract Society, 18--, p.184

4   Hants R.O. Op.Cit.

5   PRO, London, PROB 11/1175, Will of Robert Weekes

6   IWRO, IW/14, 1837.

7   Hants.R.O., 1797/A5, Will of John Barber

8   School Archives

9   IWRO, IW/14, 1837

10   PRO,London, PROB 11/1486, Will of Rev. F Worsley

11   School archives

12   C. of E. R.O., London, Returns of Select Committee on the Education of the Poor (1818), Vol.II, p.822

13   C.of E. R.O., London, Education Enquiry - Abstract of the Answers & Returns made Pursuant to an Address of the House of Commons dated 24 May 1833.

14   Portsmouth Public Library, Hants. Miscellany IV, p.234, Certificates of Dissenters Meeting Houses, Vol.6 1776-1789

15   C.of E.R.O., Education Enquiry - see (13)

16   Ibid., p.867(2)

17   Ibid. p.867 (5)

18   Encyc. Brit., Vol. 7, pp.979/80 (1951)

19   Ibid. p.980

20   Ibid.

21   IWRO IW/14, 1837

22   PRO, London, PROB 11/1942, Will of Sir Henry Worsley

23   C.of E. Education Office, Portsmouth, letter Sir H. Worsley to Rev. A. Gother.

24   School Archives

25   C. of E. Education Office, Portsmouth. Letter Sir H. Worsley to Rev. A. Gother.

26   In school archives.

27   Diocesan Schools Office, Portsmouth. Copy in School Archives.

28   C.E.R.O., London.

29   Diocesan Schools Office. Copy in School Archives.

30   Ibid.

31   Ibid.

32   I.W.R.O., 1851 Census

33   Diocesan Schools Office. Copy in School Archives.

34   Ibid.

35 Ibid.
36 A History of English Education from 1760,H.C.Barnard, London University Press, 2nd Edn., 1961, p.101.
37 School accounts. Copy in School Archives.
38 Hants. R.O., 1797/A5. Will of J. Barber.
39 In private hands, Mr. E. Roberts, Chale.
40 In private hands, Mr E Roberts, Denhams, Chale.
41 Education Act 1870, Section 14.
42 I.W.R.O., CHAL/PR/58, Minutes of Vestry Meeting.
43 Ibid
44 Ibid
45 I.W.County Press, 18 July 1891, p.8.
46 Ibid.
47 I.W.County Press, 1 August 1891.
48 In private hands, Mr E Roberts, Chale.
49 Encyclopaedia Britannica, Vol. 7, p.983, 1951.
50 In school archives.
51 Ibid.
52 Diocesan Education Office, Portsmouth. Copy in school archives.
53 Included in accounts in school archives.
54 Diocesan Education Office, Portsmouth. Copy in school archives.
55 C.of E. R.O., London. Copy in school archives.
56 I.W.R.O., 1891 Census.
57 Encyclopaedia Britannica, Vol.7, p.984, 1951.
58 I.W.R.O., CC/ED/1/2, IWCC Education Committee Minute book. p.347, 10 April, 1907.
59 In School Archives.
60 C.of E. R.O., London. Copy in School Archives.
61 In School Archives.
62 C. of E. R.O., London.
63 Ibid.
64 Encyclopaedia Britannica, Vol. 21, p.861, 1951
65 Encyclopaedia Britannica, Vol. 7, p.402/3, 1951.
66 In private hands, Mrs E. Brown, Brighstone.
67 IWRO, CC/ED/3/4, p.209, 1916.
68 Ibid, p.40
69 Ibid, p.122
70 In School Archives.
71 IWRO, CC/ED/3/4, p.241, 1916
72 Ibid, p.57
73 Ibid, p.38
74 In private hands, Mrs. E. Brown, Brighstone.

75 School Archives
76 Ibid
77 Ibid
78 I.W.County Press, 7.10.22
79 I.W.County Press 30.9.22
80 I.W.County Press 21.10.22
81 A Guide to the Educational System of England & Wales, Min. of Education Pamphlet No.2, p.51, para.18, H.M.S.O., 1945.‰
82 C.of E. R.O., letter Rev.C.W.Heald to Nat. Soc., 3.8.1920.
83 Lord Louis Library, Newport. O16/ISL/1977
    Education in Hampshire & the Isle of Wight, a Guide to Records, Ed. by C.R.Davey, Pub. Hants. Archivist Group Publication No.3, 1977, p.22.
84 Ibid.
85 Guide to the Educational System... p.17, para.48. (as 7).
86 I.W.R.O., CC/ED/1/3, p.94.
87 I.W.R.O., CC/ED/3/3, p.349; CC/ED/3/4, p.9, etc.
88 I.W.R.O., CC/ED/3/2, P.85.
89 I.W.R.O., CC/ED/3/3, p.206.
90 I.W.R.O., CC/ED/3/3, p.341, 1913
91 C.E.R.O., Letter Rev. C W Heald to National Society. Copy in School Archives.
92 Bible Christians are no longer active. Their former chapel is now a private house in Town Lane. Blackgang Mission situated in Blythe Shute, is not very active.
93 A complete list of staff can be found under "S" at the beginning of Log Book beginning Autumn Term 1966, and of Managers under "M".
94 I.W.R.O. , AC/95/25 Chale Charities' Minute Book, p.174.